The Journey of the Accidental Leader

Steve Gladis, Ph.D.

HRD Press, Inc. • Amherst • Massachusetts

Published by: HRD Press, Inc.
22 Amherst Road
Amherst, MA 01002
413-253-3488
800-822-2801 (U.S. and Canada)
413-253-3490 (fax)
www.hrdpress.com

ISBN 978-1-59996-121-7

Editorial services by Sally Farnham
Production services by Jean Miller
Cover design by Eileen Klockars

I dedicate this book to Barbara Sheehan, my 92-year-old mother-in-law, who knows as much about leadership as any CEO I have met.

Table of Contents

Introduction

Many people have written leadership books. Everyone from Tom Peters to Peter Drucker and from Rudy Giuliani to Jack Welch has offered a list of what he or she believes great leadership should be. Even researchers such as Jim Collins (author of *Good to Great* and *Built to Last*) and the folks from Gallup (*First Break All the Rules* by Buckingham and Coffman) observe, interview, and analyze great leaders to figure out what they do in order to teach new leaders a path to success.

Everyone who writes effectively about leadership has some authentic basis for the lessons he or she wants to pass on to the new generation of leaders. I'm no different. My particular, authentic "take" on my own leadership lessons has its roots in an organization that has trained some of this nation's most successful leaders: the United States Marine Corps.

In 1968, I started my own journey as an accidental leader. The war in Vietnam was still raging and the draft was in place. When I graduated from Providence College, I had two choices: (1) join the military or (2) be drafted. Breaking the law and fleeing to Canada was not a viable alternative for me. Therefore, I chose to join the U.S. Marines and found myself, the year after I graduated, in Vietnam leading troops in combat. Everything I ever learned about good leadership I learned in the Marine Corps during that difficult time. I won't say it all came naturally or easily. In fact, some of it came with great pain.

I once heard a quip: "Life happens when you're planning something else." And when it comes to leadership, it's even more true. How many of us have found ourselves looking around for leaders—someone else to take charge—when the responsibility to take action fell upon us?

Leadership is not inherited. Often the circumstances dictate whose turn it is. I call this accidental leadership. There's no grand plan; it just sort of happens, accidentally.

The fictional story that follows—a business parable—helps demonstrate some of the leadership lessons I learned in the Marine Corps. I hope it will make the journey for future accidental leaders just a bit easier. Following the story is a section called "Lessons on Leadership." I hope you enjoy the story and the lessons.

The Beginning

The phone was ringing way too early that morning, Sammy Williamson thought as he grabbed the receiver and heard his mother trying to talk over her own sobbing.

~

Samuel "Sammy" Williamson, Jr., lived in a Carmel, California, bungalow that overlooked the Pacific Ocean. By anyone's standards, even those of the movie stars who frequented the trendy seaside art colony for the rich and famous, Sammy's house drew ooh's and ah's because of its spectacular view. Just 33 years old, Sammy was tall, tanned, good looking with dark wavy hair, and smart. He'd been given his family's West Coast "cottage" at Carmel-by-the-Sea when his parents became so involved in their consulting business, Williamson Associates, in New York City, that they hadn't visited their seaside retreat in years.

Sammy, Ellen and Sam Williamson's only child, graduated from the University of Santa Barbara in film studies with a minor in business (his father had insisted on it), and Sammy often visited the Carmel cottage to relax and chill out. After a while, the house became known in the family as Sammy's place, for he had moved there after college and spent the past ten years chasing down one West Coast business venture after another—most of which came his way from his father's business connections. When he wasn't chasing business ventures, he was trying to "find himself" with continuing support from his family: traveling to Europe, dabbling in short films, and even writing and submitting a screenplay—but he never wanted to move from Carmel to either Los Angeles or New York to pursue a film career in earnest.

This particular July day, Sammy's mother called after his morning run. She was crying. His father, only 63 years old, had suffered a massive stroke and died.

Sammy grabbed the first available flight back East, and within eight hours after his shower in Carmel, he entered his parents' posh apartment on 79th and Park Avenue. His mother was sitting in her wing chair, surrounded by friends, relatives, and executives from the firm, but when she saw her son, she rose and walked toward him, then fell into his arms, sobbing.

"Sammy, it's so terrible. Oh my God. I can't believe it."

Fighting a flood of tears himself, Sammy asked her what had happened.

"Dad was running around the reservoir in the Park...he fell. They tried to help. Took him to the hospital. It was awful," she said, dissolving into Sammy's arms.

The next few days were full of the difficult business of death. The wake, the funeral, testimonials at the church, the burial; the sorrow, tears, his mother's wails at night; the family, relatives, and friends. And then, there was the business itself.

For years, to no avail, Sammy's father had tried to get him interested in returning to the East Coast and joining their consulting business. When he was a boy, Sammy's father had brought him into the business to meet the people and see how his father made a living. In high school, Sammy had shadowed his father as part of an honors program — only to summarize his time with Dad at the office as "boring." During his summer college breaks, Sammy had worked in the firm to earn college spending money but used much of his time wishing he was doing something — anything — else. In short, all his father's attempts to interest Sammy in the family business had backfired and produced a West Coaster out of an East Coast kid.

It was his great uncle, Joe Williamson, who gave Sammy what was to become life-changing news at the luncheon reception for family and close friends following the burial at the family plot in Westchester. Brother to Sammy's grandfather, Uncle Joe had always been old — even since Sam was a young boy. Small, thin, and balding, Joe had only wisps of gray hair to remind him of the black waves he'd sported when he was in his 30s. Of all his relatives, Sammy had always been closest to his Uncle Joe, now in his late 70s, because he was so wise and candid. Well, blunt was a better word for it.

After swallowing a bite of Italian cannoli and looking over his black-framed glasses, Uncle Joe looked straight at Sammy and asked, "So, Sammy, what are you going to do about the business?"

"Business?" Sammy asked, genuinely confused.

"The family business."

"What about it?"

"The consulting firm that your Dad left to you."

"Left to me?"

"Yes."

"Uncle Joe, what the heck are you talking about?"

"You really don't know?"

The Letter

The three of them sat in the living room of the large Park Avenue apartment, Sammy on the couch with his Uncle Joe, and Ellen, Sammy's mother, in her favorite blue wing chair. Slight, with graying brown hair, Ellen had a vacant look in her eyes. The large brown leather chair—his father's chair—sat empty.

"Mom, just when were you going to tell me?"

"Sammy, easy now," said Uncle Joe.

"Look, I know this has been a difficult time, but really, when did you plan on letting me know, Mom?"

Without saying a word, Sammy's mother pulled out a brown business envelope from her tote bag, which was resting next to her chair on the hardwood floor, and handed it to Sammy. It had not been sealed, which struck Sammy as a bit strange, but it did have his name printed on the outside. Sammy recognized the distinctive left-handed slant of his father's writing and the purple ink he'd used his entire life. A "purple note" at the firm meant that it came directly from Sam, Sr., and demanded immediate attention.

In absolute quiet, Sammy read the one-page letter to himself.

Sammy,

I know this letter may not make you happy. Hopefully that will change in time. However, I'm directing you to run the business upon my death. If you're reading this, something has happened to me. Your mother is grieving and needs no more on her plate—so don't make this difficult for her or your Uncle Joe. This was my idea—not theirs.

You are to run the firm for one year. If at the end of that year you decide to sell it, you must first offer it to the employees to buy it. If they don't want to buy the firm, you can sell it to any number of companies that will be taking a run at buying it very soon, believe me. The decision will be yours.

However, you must run the company for one year. To help you run it, I've asked Uncle Joe to be your confidant and coach. He's the wisest man I know; he will teach you all you need to lead the company. I know this isn't what you wanted, but I'm asking you to take on the responsibility.

At the end of one year, you can go back to California or wherever you like, and half the proceeds from the sale of the company will be yours. Your mother will get the other half. At current valuation, the company is worth between $20 and $30 million. If on the other hand you decide not to take on this challenge, you'll receive no more money from the estate, the property in Carmel will be sold, and you'll be on your own to find a job and fend for yourself.

While I suspect you may be confused now and may not be able to understand why I've done this, I hope one day you'll understand it all. In the meantime, good luck and don't forget to ask Uncle Joe for his advice. He's a wise man and loves you, almost as much as your mother and I do.

Love always,

Dad

When he finished the letter, Sammy was tempted to crumple it up and toss it into the trash, but he remembered his father's words: "... your Mother is grieving and needs no more on her plate..."

Uncle Joe spoke first. "Sammy, both your mother and I will support you. But I think for now, it's best that we don't talk today. Tomorrow, I suggest you come to my apartment so we can begin. I'll have a couple of bagels and coffee ready."

With some effort, Joe got to his feet, walked over and kissed Sammy's mother on the cheek, and patted her shoulder softly as she began to cry.

"It will be all right, Ellen, time will heal all wounds." Then, Joe walked to Sammy, patted him on the shoulder, kissed him on the cheek, and headed for the door.

Lesson Number One:
On Trying

Uncle Joe's apartment was a one-bedroom in midtown Manhattan on the corner of 33rd and Third Avenue. From his balcony you could look out in one direction at the Empire State Building and in another direction see the Chrysler Building. The commanding view more than made up for the compactness of Joe's apartment. Both Sammy and Joe sat at the table a full minute before Sammy spoke.

"I can't do this, Uncle Joe."

Joe just stared, sipped his coffee, and chewed his bagel.

"I'm serious. This afternoon, I'm going to book a flight back to the West Coast. I can't do this."

Joe continued to eat.

"Aren't you going to say anything, Uncle Joe?"

"Goodbye," Joe said, waving his bony, veined left hand before returning it to his coffee cup.

"That's it, goodbye?"

"What are you expecting from me when you tell me you will not respect your father's final wishes—a pat on the back? Maybe a going-away present?"

"Listen, I never asked for this." Sammy walked into the tiny kitchen for more coffee.

"Fine—then, goodbye."

"I have trouble running my own life, let alone a company," Sammy said, with an exaggerated shrug of his broad shoulders and his hands palms up.

"You think your father knew anything when he got started?"

"What?" Sammy looked perplexed.

"Your father didn't have a pot to pee into or a window to throw it out of. Your mother was pregnant with you;

they were broke — we all were. So he started to help out companies with writing advertising copy because your mother told him once that he could write well."

"I never knew that. They never told me. Ever since I could remember, we've been...well off."

"There's a lot they never told you, Sammy," Joe said, reaching for the napkin.

"What else?"

"**Lesson number one in business: No one knows what they're doing until they try,**" Joe said, staring directly at Sammy.

"What do you mean?"

"Just what I said. You think Henry Ford knew what he was doing until he tried it? Or Edison, Jefferson, take any of them. Everyone starts out by taking the first step and cutting a new trail as they go along. There's no easy guide or script. You write your own adventure as you go, Sammy."

"What about business school?" Sammy was rubbing his forehead as if to massage out another idea.

"Another excuse to stay in the womb for a couple more years. Like law school — a finishing school for uncommitted liberal arts graduates. Better to go into the army — at least you'll learn discipline. Business school? You think Carnegie, Rockefeller, Ford went to business school? Maybe you think Shakespeare or Hemmingway got their master's degrees in creative writing?"

"But I have no clue about what my father's company does."

"So study. Even in California they teach you how to study, don't they?"

"Yes, of course."

"So go to work and figure it out. And, remember **Lesson number one: "No one knows what they're doing until they try."**

Sammy nodded slowly, but Uncle Joe knew he had not quite gotten it. So he decided to take out a piece of paper and write a note on it. He handed it to Sammy and said, "Here, whatever you decide, this is something to keep in your wallet."

Sammy took the card, looked intently at it, and asked, "So, what does this mean $-L = RT, RT, RR$?"

"Simple. It's my formula for success $-$ Leaders do the Right Thing, at the Right Time, and for the Right Reason."

The First Day

On Sammy's first day on the job, he got lost. He had written down the wrong address and ended up on East 76th Street instead of East 67th Street. Consequently, when he went to hit the elevator button for the 20th floor and saw that the building's floors stopped at 15, he checked the return address on the letter his father had sent him, realized his error, hopped into a cab, and headed for 67th.

That day his father's longtime executive assistant, Mary Martell, showed him around the office. Mary was a slight woman with short brown hair and blonde highlights, maybe 45 or 50 years old, and walked with a self-assured gait. The tour lasted about a half hour and covered both the 20th and 21st floors of the building. A few people bustled about. However, Mary explained, most were on site at various client businesses, and so the office appeared understaffed and quiet.

"Right here is your office, Sammy...," she started to say, then amending herself quickly, "I mean, Mr. Williamson." It was difficult because Sammy's father had brought him into the office for many years, and Mary had watched over him whenever his father had to step out of the office for a moment. In effect, she had been Sammy's babysitter, so, having her call him Mr. Williamson seemed artificial at best.

"Mary, please call me Sam, okay?"

She nodded and smiled at Sammy, then gave him a large notebook to read. It was an overview of the company his father had pulled together once, when he had thought about selling the business.

Sammy went into his office and read the notebook with intense interest, hoping to find some answers but ultimately guessing that Uncle Joe was right—experience would just happen. That's when his phone rang with his first problem as the CEO.

"Hello, this is Sam Williamson," he said, feeling quite awkward sitting in his father's chair and answering the phone using his father's name.

"Sam? Who?" a gruff voice asked.

"Sam, Jr. How can I help you?"

"This is Al Bolton," the man said, and then paused for a second as if to catch his breath. "I got this kid—Sean Jacobs—from your company working on my ad campaign. He's about the same age as my grandson."

Sammy paused to think about how his father might handle this situation, and then said, "If you're not happy, I'll replace him today." Sammy paused to look back at something his father had written in the notebook: "Focus on the client, always." Then he said, "In fact, I'll come over myself AND won't charge you a penny for our service if you're not happy at the end of the day. Deal?"

"Okay. That's fair."

On his first official mission as a CEO, Sammy got the address from Mary, jumped in a cab, and headed downtown to Al Bolton's offices in lower Manhattan.

After nearly six hours of working in a cramped Bolton Associates' office with Sean Jacobs, the young Williamson copywriter who had been assigned the Bolton account, Sammy squeezed the bridge of his nose and looked up at the clock. "Well, Sean, I think we've got things under control now. Al's an impatient old guy. You already had most of the campaign developed before I got here. Just needed a little refining."

"Thanks for bailing me out, Boss. I thought he was going to throw me out the friggin' window."

"No problem," Sammy said as he thought about what the young man had called him: Boss.

Later on his way home, Sammy stopped by his Uncle Joe's apartment—as much to check up on Joe as to talk to him about his first day as the CEO. It was a hot August evening, and Joe had all the windows open and a fan working.

"Uncle Joe, why don't you turn on the air conditioning? It's hot as hell."

"I don't waste electricity. When it gets very hot, I'll use it."

Sammy slapped his head with one hand and mopped his brow with the other, "Yeah, I hear it's going to get hot tomorrow! No sense wasting the kilowatts on today."

Uncle Joe nodded in somber agreement and asked, "So, how was the first day on the job?" He poured Sammy a glass of ice water.

"Eventful. I met Al Bolton," Sammy said, and he began to recount his day after Bolton's phone call.

"That old pain in the ass. He used to drive your father nuts. Always with the complaints about this or that. Didn't matter. If Al was breathing, he was complaining. A regular crank," Joe said, and wiped the sweat from his forehead with the red bandana he kept handy.

With that, Sammy explained his remedy and how he'd worked with Sean, the young associate, for six hours; how Sammy promised Al a money-back guarantee; how he'd gone to Al's office and waited while Al reviewed the work and finally agreed that he was satisfied and would pay for the job.

"Praise God in the heavens. That pain in the neck. It used to take your father months to collect from him—such a cheapskate—I'm talking about Al, of course."

Sammy laughed out loud.

"Sammy. You see what I'm saying, **"Lesson number one in business: No one knows what they're doing until they try."**

Sammy nodded and sipped the ice water.

"And, Sammy, you acted like a real leader. You did the Right Thing, at the Right Time, and for the Right Reason."

Lesson Number Two:
On Giving

The next day, Sammy made no mistakes finding the building and came into the office right at 9:00 a.m., as his father had done for 40 years. Mary was already hard at work, and the office bustled with a few more people than the day before. Several people said hello to Sammy on his way in and smiled with a kind of generosity he had not expected.

"You had quite a day at Mr. Bolton's, I heard," Mary said to Sammy when he picked up his messages and started to move toward his office.

He stopped to look at her. "Heard what?"

"Let's just say a little bird told me how you handled Aching Al—I mean Mr. Bolton—pretty well."

"Aching Al?" Sammy laughed.

"That's one of the kinder names your dad called Mr. Bolton. I won't repeat several others he used to describe him," Mary said, beginning to blush.

"Could that little bird be Sean Jacobs?"

"No, actually Al's assistant and I have become friends over the years. She's been sweeping up his messes for a long time."

"So, what's on tap for today? As he spoke, Sammy looked at the silver-framed photo of Mary with his father on Mary's desk. Taken almost 20 years ago, the photo gave Sammy's heart a brief twinge.

"On Tuesdays your dad had regular senior staff meetings with George Garber and Vince Oliveri."

"George and Vince, sure, I remember them. They're still here?"

"Oh, yes," she said, "Still here."

"And?"

"I'll let you make up your own mind," she said, and with that she pointed her nose and eyes back to her computer screen.

At 9:30 a.m. sharp, a short, portly, bald, and florid-faced, 65-year-old George Garber knocked on Sammy's door and entered his office without waiting for a reply.

"Sammy, how are you, son?" His right hand jutted forward for a shake.

"George, good to see you." Sammy rose and walked out in front of his large mahogany desk to take George's hand firmly. Then he motioned George toward the two brown leather chairs near the window overlooking the city.

"So sorry about your father, Sammy," George said. He tightened his lips and looked down at the oriental rug for just a moment.

"Thanks, I appreciate that very much, George." After a pause, Sammy said, "Ah, I prefer...at work I'd prefer to go by Sam, not Sammy."

"Oh, pardon me...Sammy—ah, Sam. Sure, sure," George said looking a bit embarrassed.

They sat and chatted for a bit until finally Sammy noted it was 9:45 and buzzed Mary. "Where's Vince?"

"He called and said he was caught in traffic."

"I see. When did he call?"

"About 10 minutes ago."

"Okay. We'll talk later. Thanks."

Sammy turned to George. "Let's start the meeting."

"But Vince will be coming in soon. He's always late. You just have to give him a time earlier than you want to start. Then he's on time."

"I'd prefer to get started."

And with that, Sammy's first executive staff meeting began. George told Sammy all the doom and gloom. The market was down, sales were down, morale was down, and so was George, on almost any subject. Now Sammy remembered that years ago when he had visited his father's office, that George was constantly reading the obituaries and always had the latest information on the day's threatening weather. Hurricane, snowstorm, or intense summer heat, George was ready to fret about it and upset everyone else in the process. Some of the more junior staff had given to calling him Gloomy George (but never to his face). Yet George had been Sam, Sr.'s, first hire when he'd started the business. And as grumpy and gloomy as George was, he was smart and loyal. As chief operating officer, he knew how to get things done, which had freed Sammy's father to find new business and make strategic partners for the firm.

When George was finished reporting on the state of the business, Sammy looked at him and said, "Is that it?"

"Well, I suppose, but how about a cup of coffee? We'll chat a bit, like Sam and I used to do."

"Look, George, I've got a lot going on. If that's all, I'll see you later."

At that moment, if you had watched George's face, you would have seen a whole range of emotion played out in a millisecond. First, his brow crunched into an angry furrow, then he clenched his teeth, grimacing.

But Sammy wasn't watching. Finally, George looked down at his notes and said, "Sure."

About 15 minutes after George left, 60-year-old, tall, thin, disheveled, and bespeckled Vince Oliveri burst into Sammy's office. "Sammy, I'm so sorry. The traffic."

Sammy was on the phone and refused to acknowledge Vince's presence. When the conversation was finished, he put down the phone, looked up at Vince, the chief financial officer who had kept his father's business running well in the black for more than 30 years, and said flatly, "Vince, you're late."

"The traffic, Sammy."

"I go by Sam now."

"Sure, Sam. I apologize."

"Please be prompt next time."

"Sure. Do you want me to go over the financials?'

"No, just leave them."

"But, I could just…"

"No thanks, not now."

Vince slipped the file onto Sammy's desk, shook his hand, and left, looking like a dog who had just been scolded.

Sammy's first executive meeting had not gone well.

Later that afternoon when Sammy returned from lunch, he noticed that Mary was more quiet than usual. She was pleasant but not quite as forthcoming as she had been previously.

"You okay?" Sammy asked.

"Fine."

"That bad, eh?"

She laughed but sobered her look quickly.

"Talk to me, Mary."

At first she spoke slowly, but then as Sammy sat in the chair next to her desk, she began to open up, "George and Vince are two characters, I will admit. Both of them need some prodding occasionally, and your dad did that when necessary. But both have served this company and your dad well for decades."

She paused to measure her next words. "Look, I talked to George and Vince separately after their meetings with you, and frankly they both felt deflated and underappreciated." She sipped the cup of water on her desk. "You know," she said, and paused again, "they're also grieving the loss of your father...just like me."

"I see. Of course," said Sammy, encouraging her to go on. And she did for another few minutes while Sammy listened intently, not saying a word.

After she finished, he asked, "Anything else?"

"No, I don't think so," she said, dabbing the corner of her right eye with a tissue.

"I'm hearing that you sound frustrated. That accurate?"

"I suppose."

"So, what do you recommend?"

"Me?"

"Yes."

"Give them some time."

"Ahh."

"George can be a grump and Vince is always late—which screws up every meeting."

"So what do you suggest I do?" Sammy leaned forward in his chair like a student listening to a professor giving a review before an exam.

"Maybe thank them for their service to your dad but remind them you have your own requirements, too. Be nice but stick to your guns."

"Okay, thanks."

Sammy started back to his office desk, then turned and said, "By the way Mary, I appreciate all you've done for me...and for my dad."

"You're welcome," she said with a faint smile.

Later that day, Sammy stopped by to see both George and Vince and individually thanked them for their service to his father, then asked them for their continued help and guidance. George grinned like a Cheshire cat. And when Sammy left Vince's office, he thought he saw Vince, who had lost his wife to cancer a year ago, brush back a tear.

On the way home that night, Sammy stopped by Uncle Joe's apartment with a corned beef sandwich from Joe's favorite deli. The two of them sat at Joe's kitchen table with the sandwich and pickles and chips spread all over the white wrapping paper as they ate and talked. Still the air conditioning was turned off and the fan turned on high.

"I thought you were going to turn on the air conditioning today."

"Maybe tomorrow when it gets hotter."

"You said that yesterday, and it's hotter today!"

"Yeah but tomorrow's supposed to get really hot."

Sammy just threw his hands in the air, "Really hot. Like this is cool?"

"Let's get back to business. How goes it?" Joe said now, munching on a large kosher dill pickle.

"I met with George and Vince."

"Ah, Mutt and Jeff," Joe said.

"Who?"

"You're too young to remember. Maybe you remember Laurel and Hardy?"

"Weren't they comics?"

"How about Beavis and Butthead?"

"Ah."

"So, was George a regular Doctor Doom, and was Vince late?"

"Bingo."

"Look, they've got their issues, but they're valuable and need to be respected."

"Mary gave me the same message."

"Yeah, but respect doesn't mean a free pass," Joe said, waving the stub of the pickle as he gestured.

"Oh?"

"Look, your father. I loved the man. You know that."

Sammy nodded, crunching down on a big potato chip.

"But those two, well, took advantage. Your father put a high premium on loyalty. And George and Vince are both loyal."

"Frankly, they're like two old ladies. And when they talk to me it's like they're talking to their son," Sammy said.

"That's because to them, you are."

"So how do I handle them?"

"Lesson number two: You get what you give. So give a little first."

"And that means…what?"

"If you want to get respect, you have to give it. If you want to get information from people, give them information. It's all about opening the door first."

"Okay. I'll bite. What's opening the door first mean?"

Uncle Joe settled back in his chair and looked out the window at the Empire State Building. "New York has a lot of big buildings. I used to work in one in the financial district in lower Manhattan," he said. "You know how they have two sets of doors to keep out the heat in summer and the cold in winter?"

Sammy nodded.

"So, whenever I got to the outside door before the people right behind me, I used to hold the door for them to go in before me. My mother taught me always to be polite. God rest her soul."

Sammy smiled.

"So, what I noticed was that whenever I held open the door first, then the next thing I know, the person who was behind me is holding open the second set of doors for me. Happened almost every time I did it. Like clockwork."

"So when didn't it?"

"Whenever a rude jerk went through!"

Sammy nodded, smiled, and took another bite of his sandwich.

"So, lesson number two: You get what you give. So give a little first."

Sammy took out a notebook he'd bought that day, turned to the first page, and started writing down some notes.

"What are you writing?" Uncle Joe asked.

"Notes on our conversation."

"What, like this is a class?" Joe said, shrugging his shoulders.

"In a way. I'm just writing down the lessons. See," he said, pushing his notebook toward Joe.

The page in the small spiral notebook read:

Lessons Learned

1. No one knows what they're doing until they try.
2. You get what you give. So give a little first.

Joe smiled, sat down, bit into the last of his sandwich, and wiped his mouth.

Lesson Number Three: On Trust

One night Sammy was awakened by a dream—the same one he'd had the night before. He'd dreamt that his father, Sam, had returned and asked him what he was doing. But when Sammy tried to speak, no words came out, no matter how much he struggled. This only frustrated his father, so he talked louder and louder until he was screaming at Sammy. Still Sammy had no voice. The dream became so animated that when Sammy awoke, he had soaked his pillow with sweat and had to turn it over before he lay his head back down. As weeks passed, despite an occasional upsetting dream or two, Sammy settled into the job. And in the month that it had taken Sammy to establish a comfortable routine, a certain unease had crept into the company culture—which had been hard-driving and no-nononsense under his father's tenure.

One morning when Mary brought in some paperwork for signature, Sammy stopped her. "Mary, can I ask you a question?"

"Sure."

"You have an ear close to the ground around the office, don't you?"

"I'd say I'm aware of office chatter if that's what you mean."

"So, then, what's the mood around the company?"

Mary hesitated to answer and looked off toward the window, then back at Sammy, then back toward the window. Finally, she settled her gaze back toward Sammy.

"May I sit down for a moment?"

"Of course."

She drew her chair right up to the edge of Sammy's desk, leaned in, and said, "Frankly, I'm concerned about the rumors going around."

"Rumors?"

"People are concerned."

"About what?"

Mary paused for a long time and then said, "You."

"Me?" Sammy said, with a deeply quizzical look.

"They don't know where you're coming from—well, actually, they don't know where you're going."

"Welcome to my world. I'm not sure either."

"I know you didn't ask for this job, but you've got it. And people are watching and waiting. Depending on you."

"For what?"

"Some direction. They're scared."

"Scared of what?" Sammy asked. He shifted in his seat and leaned forward. "I've been called a few things in my life, but never scary."

"They're not afraid of you...just the situation," she said. "They're not sure if they can trust you."

Sammy's eyes narrowed and he gritted his teeth as he felt the flush of anger rise into his face. "I can't believe this. Trust me?"

Mary drew back instinctively. "Maybe I used the wrong word. They're just unsure of what direction you're going. Where the company's headed. Where their careers are going."

"I need to digest all this, Mary."

"Sure, I didn't mean to upset you, but you asked."

"Of course, thanks. I just need some time," Sammy said, as the anger in him subsided.

She nodded, took some papers back with her, and shut the door. That day whenever he wasn't in one meeting or another, Sammy thought about what Mary had said. And right before he left for the day, Sammy called Uncle Joe and asked to meet him at a local diner that he knew Joe liked.

Eddie's Diner on the corner of 34th and Lexington Avenue had been a favorite haunt of Joe's. He'd worked and lived in the same neighborhood for years and remained loyal to Eddie's and to its chef and owner, Eddie Krabowski.

After they had ordered, Sammy told Joe about the trust issue that Mary had raised at work earlier that day. Just as Joe started to respond, the two of them heard a booming voice from behind the marble counter.

"Hey, Joe," yelled Eddie, all decked out in his black-and-white checkered pants, white starched shirt, and grand chef's hat. A rotund, bearded man who looked like a great French chef, Eddie walked over to the table and grabbed Joe's hand like it was the last time two great friends would meet.

"Eddie, you old sea dog. Good to see you—sober!"

"This from the kind of guy who used to make wine in his own cellar!"

Both of the men roared—it was a standing joke because both had been through Alcoholics Anonymous and clean and sober for more than 30 years. After the amenities and some chit chat, Eddie got back to the kitchen. Joe turned to Sammy and said, "Now, that's a stand-up guy—one you *can trust*."

"How so?"

"When it comes to trust, it's all about the five Cs: character, competence, caring, commitment, and consistency."

"Interesting."

"Let me hit the high points, then give you an example. First, character. That boils down to honesty. If I can rely on what you say, that you do what you say you'll do, and if you don't, you'll make it right—then I say you've got character."

"I see."

"Everything else is related, but honesty sets the base for all the other values like integrity, responsibility, ambition, and all the rest."

"Okay, so what about competence?"

"You have to be good at the basic business you're leading so that people will listen to you and have confidence in what you say. That means you have to master your profession to be taken seriously," Joe said, and then took a sip of water and pointed at Eddie.

"Like to run a restaurant, Eddie has to at least know how to cook."

"Exactly. Even if you're not the best cook in the place, you still need to know how to be a cook—a competent one—to have the respect of your team."

"That makes sense, but I think I'll stay away from cooking and stick to consulting."

"Having tasted your cooking, I'd agree, Sammy! But the next one—caring—needs to be central to anything you do when dealing with people. If people feel that you genuinely care about them and their families, there's nothing they wouldn't do for you."

Sammy fingered the paper napkin and looked at the silverware in front of him as he thought to himself. Then he said, "I remember in high school when I worked at a summer job for a distribution company on the West Side. Mom got sick, and I had to spend some time helping her get to doctor appointments. The supervisor, Mr. Smellings, told me to do what I had to and that he'd handle my absence. I'll never forget him telling me that my mother was the most important thing in my life then, not the job."

"Sounds like Mr. Smellings was a first-rate leader."

"I still send him a holiday card to this day. He's the only boss I still correspond with."

"So I rest my case about the power of caring. Now, finally, let's take commitment and consistency. I take these two together because they're both about integrity—living up to promises. Look—if you're inconsistent or refuse to commit to a plan of action, people see you as unreliable at best, and nuts at worst."

"Huh?"

"Think about it. The most inconsistent people in the world are mentally ill—we even call them mentally imbalanced. If you commit to a course of action at the company, you need to live up to your pledge. If you want the respect of your followers and others, you have to take the first step and stay on course for the entire journey, or it will not work," Joe said as the waiter served their food.

"Okay, so how's all this apply to Eddie?" As he spoke, Sammy looked over at the diner owner behind the counter.

"For more than 30 years I've been coming here. During that time, I've seen a lot of employees come and go," Joe said. "Some were students, others between careers, some who didn't fit the culture, and all the rest. Through it all, Eddie's been the best leader I've ever met." He dug into his eggs and corned beef hash.

There was a lull in the conversation. Sammy ate some of his scrambled eggs and ham with rye toast, and as he did so, he kept eyeing Eddie behind the counter. He had his arm around one of the waiters and was laughing with the waiter and one of the customers.

Joe sipped a steaming mug of hot coffee and noticed Sammy's glance. After he wiped his mouth with his napkin, Joe said, "There was this woman from El Salvador. Immigration—INS—wanted to deport her. She'd come to work for Eddie after her no-good husband deserted her and their baby. Then when he gets in trouble, to save his own skin, the jerk husband turns her in to Immigration. She'd forgotten to register, or some snafu, and INS was on one of their compliance kicks. I guess they needed a statistic for a report. Anyway, they demanded that she be turned over for deportation, or they'd close down the diner, arrest her, and arrest Eddie."

Sammy sipped his coffee and leaned in closer to Joe. "So, what the heck could Eddie do?"

"Turns out that one time a new church was starting up in the city and asked Eddie if they could rent the diner on Sunday morning for church until they got enough money to build or rent a larger church. For years, Eddie didn't open until noon on Sundays, so he agreed to rent to the new church for nothing. He charged them a dollar a year to make it legal and gave them the keys to the place. Even let them get their mail here. So in effect, the diner becomes a house of worship."

"You've got to be kidding. Let me guess. Eddie claims the diner as a place of sanctuary, which prohibits INS from grabbing the woman as long as she's on the premises!"

"Bingo, Sammy, you're a smart kid," Joe said, pointing his finger at Sammy.

"Yeah, but how?"

"He sets up a room in the back of the store for the woman and her son and stares down Immigration."

"I'm surprised they didn't either intimidate him or tie him up in court."

"Eddie's the best cook in the city. He knows a lot of influential people, including lawyers, many of whom studied for their law school and bar exams in the back of this diner and ate stacks of pancakes and drank vats of coffee for free when they were broke. So, a couple of Eddie's Diner law fellows stepped in to help him, and they tied up the INS—instead of the other way around."

"So, what happened?"

"The woman gets a green card, Eddie gets an award from the Latino community, and her kid gets to finish school, goes to NYU—and becomes a friggin' immigration lawyer—HA!" Joe said, slamming the table with his right hand.

Sammy roared—not only from the punchline of the story but also from watching Joe's reaction to his own story, which Sammy figured he'd told a few hundred times in his life.

Just then as if on cue, Eddie, still behind the counter, also roared. He'd been talking to one of his waitresses, who was obviously laughing at something he'd said.

Joe looked at Sammy over his reading glasses like a professor and asked, "So, how about trust? Did Eddie hit the five Cs—character, competence, caring, commitment, and consistency?"

Sammy smiled, nodded, and said, "So I guess we're at lesson number three now?"

"Yep. **Lesson number three: Build trust by character, competence, caring, commitment, and consistency.**"

Joe winked at Sammy and jotted down on a napkin: L = RT, RT, RR. Sammy remembered: *Leaders do the right thing, at the right time, for the right reason.* He nodded again, took out his notebook, opened it, and added a third lesson to his growing list:

Lessons Learned

1. No one knows what they're doing until they try.

2. You get what you give. So give a little first.

3. Build trust by character, competence, caring, commitment, and consistency.

Joe smiled as he looked at Sammy writing and asked, "Now, how about some apple pie?"

The Meeting

Sammy took off the next day of work. He called Mary early and told her that he needed to work on a project and would be at his apartment if she or anyone needed him. Generally a very private person, Sammy needed "alone time" more than most people, because lots of people and chatter often wore him down. It wasn't that he disliked people. However, gatherings of people tended to sap his energy. He was fine with one or two people at a time — especially if he knew them. But lots of people, all needing air time with him, drained his energy.

So, he relished this time to be with the single person he trusted the most — himself. He considered what Uncle Joe had said about Eddie and about building trust and thought about how important that was, especially given his new role.

New role, he thought. Exactly. It was a role. We all play roles, he mused. Sometimes we're put in charge of a project, other times we're the followers. But we do play roles. This was Sammy's new role — leader.

But he thought the role had to be played from an authentic place, not some fabricated one — as if he were in some high school play. He remembered the five Cs that Uncle Joe told him were the keys to building trust: character, competence, caring, commitment, and consistency. It was like Sammy had been put in charge of an important combat mission after his leader was killed in action. He had to be ready with the right stuff at the right time, and be ready to assume the role of platoon leader. As he followed his thoughts, Sammy drew further and further inside himself — his favorite place to be when solving problems.

After a couple of hours of jotting down notes, Sammy took a break. He put down his pen, leaned back on the couch, and let his mind drift into a pleasant meditation — somewhere between sleep and wakefulness. Floating in that drifting place, he felt weightless, even thought-less — free from the world. About 20 minutes later, when he awoke, he felt like the cluttered chalkboard of his mind had been cleaned.

That's when he thought of his idea — **The Trust Exercise.** Quickly he moved to his computer, pulled up a blank e-mail form, and started typing.

Dear Colleagues,

Tomorrow at 10:30 a.m. I'd like us all to meet. Here's what I'd like you to come prepared to discuss:

1. **Your three or four strongest personal abilities.** Maybe you're very analytical or perhaps strategic. Or maybe you're great at building personal relationships, making people laugh, or being a strong leader.

2. **The areas that challenge you.** You might not be good with data analysis or not like to work on teams; perhaps you take things too personally and get hurt; or maybe you're not as experienced as you'd like.

3. **I'll do the same and will be the first to share** my strengths and challenges with the group.

Thanks,

Sam

The next morning when Sammy entered the large conference room next to his office, he saw a group of people talking, laughing, and kidding with each other. Many of them were pointing out their lists to friends who nodded and smiled. Some were more somber and held their papers or notebooks close to themselves. The nervous energy had a kind of electricity to it. But as he moved toward the front of the gathering, the room became as quiet as an empty church.

"Well, I guess I sure can stop a good time!" he said. People laughed, and that helped Sammy's confidence. "Look, I've only been here a short time and have not gotten to talk with all of you yet. But I thought this might be a good time for us to really get to know each other more personally. Frankly, I believe if you're ever going to trust me, you have to know more about what makes me tick."

Sammy looked around for any reaction. So far, so good, he thought. "When I sent my e-mail yesterday, I'm guessing that some of you thought—what a kook!" Some of the employees laughed, and a few even nodded. Sammy pointed to the nodders and said, "At least there are some very honest folks here."

He paused before going on so that he wouldn't get too emotional. "My dad was a great guy. I loved him a lot as I know you all did in your own ways."

Sammy cleared his throat and continued, "I am not my dad. He was a real outgoing guy. The man never met a stranger. Would talk to a lamppost." A great roar of nervous laughter erupted, followed by exaggerated nodding from the crowd, which made Sammy and the crowd feel much better.

"I'm more of a one-on-one person and not nearly as outgoing as Dad. So I'm a pretty good listener—not such a great conversationalist at parties or a chit-chatterer. In that way, I'm more like my mother, who listened to my Dad for years—boy did she listen!" More laughter.

Sammy continued, "For as much as my dad loved to talk, he always told me to listen to others, value their abilities, and respect their opinions. And you all know my Uncle Joe, who's become my mentor as I get used to this job."

There, he thought, he'd admitted what everyone in the company knew—that Joe was Sammy's appointed managerial guardian. "Look, I make no apologies for having to learn this business, and Joe has been a great teacher, along with all of you. And I pledge to listen to everything you have to teach me," he said.

With that Sammy got up and moved toward a flip chart, wrote his name, and printed the word "Strengths" at the top of the page. Then under that he wrote the words "Good listener" and put down the marker. He remained standing and held the yellow pad with his notes on it.

"Dad was a real strategist—could always see the big picture—was a real vision guy," Sammy said. "Remember when he came up with his idea for 'continuous consulting'? He got the firm on regular retainers with a number of firms and charged them on a simple sliding scale that allowed them to access us cheaply for quick answers to simple day-to-day problems, which led to more advanced and more highly compensated work—what a great idea… the man had vision." People around the room smiled.

"I'm more analytical. I like to take things apart and see how they work. I'm good at finding solutions and putting puzzles together. So, if you're ever working on a jigsaw puzzle, call me up." He wrote the second item under Strengths: "Analytical."

People leaned forward, their eyes locked on Sammy. "Look, I think a good business is like having a Thanksgiving dinner, where everyone brings different specialty dishes they've prepared. Or, in the case of business, they've brought their varied and valued abilities to the table. My dad had a natural ability for strategy, so he brought that gift to this company's table. But someone else in the firm had to bring the analysis to bear to help execute that strategy. I suspect George and Vince helped out in that department," he said looking in their direction, as they smiled, almost embarrassed.

"Placing a high value on the diversity and talent that each person brings to a team is something Dad taught me to do. He used to say to me, 'Sammy, a quarterback is only as good as his linemen, running backs, and receivers—the whole damned offensive team! And he doesn't even get to touch the ball if special teams and his defense don't work.'

"Dad taught me to value everyone and to care deeply about the individual personal and professional success of everyone in the company." Sammy stopped to take a sip of water. He'd been feeling emotion beginning to surge within him. He needed to collect himself.

"Next, my dad had a huge heart. Anyone who ever came to him with a problem knew how he took it personally. He wore his heart on his sleeve. You knew where he was emotionally all the time. And he made all of his decisions based on emotions…his gut," Sammy said as he looked at George and Vince, who were seated together near the front of the group. Both of them looked at each other and nodded and rolled their eyes as if to say: *And how!*

"Now I'd be the first to tell you how much I admire my dad's ability to make good decisions using his gut that way, but I'm different. I'm a real logical guy. I don't get as tied up with emotions. I make more fact-based decisions, which can sometimes appear cool and impersonal, but I'm more comfortable making decisions that way," he said. He moved to the chart and wrote "Logical" in the Strengths column.

"But Dad did teach me to be committed to whatever I decided to do — and not to be afraid to take a stand — to act consistently and dependably with that decision. I remember one time in college when one of my friends ran for class president. I agreed to be his campaign manager, but as the campaign wore on, and other candidates I knew threw their hats in the ring, and as the semester's classes got harder, I lost my fervor a bit. I fortunately told Dad about it over Thanksgiving break. Man, did I get a lecture about staying the course and living up to my word. I never forgot that lesson and don't intend to now. So, please hold me to my commitment to this company, and if you ever see me waver, let me know. Starting today, in order to demonstrate my commitment to you, I'm placing several anonymous suggestion boxes around the company, where I'd like you to leave typed and unsigned messages for me about any thoughts you might have — either positive or negative. I promise to personally empty the boxes every Friday and address your concerns — myself."

George glanced at Mary and then at Vince with a look that said *What the hell is this all about?* Mary answered both of them with several shoulder shrugs, as if to say *I have no idea!*

When Sammy moved away from the chart, he looked down at his yellow pad and said, "My dad was a get-it-done guy. In fact, I think he must have helped Nike come up with their slogan — 'Just Do It.' He lived by the clock.

And deadlines, yikes." A number of people chuckled. "If Dad told you to meet him at a certain time, you'd better be there 10 minutes early.

"I'm more like my mother. I'm a take-life-as-it comes guy. I prefer to play first, and work later. As most of you know, I spent more than a few years in Carmel exploring my business and professional options, shall we say. I'm pretty good at researching because I do look for options — don't lock in to anything too fast. My father would testify to that," he said, laughing aloud at himself.

He moved toward the chart and wrote the words "Good at researching options."

So the chart looked like this:

Sam Williamson

Strengths:

1. Good listener
2. Analytical
3. Logical
4. Good at researching options

Then he drew a sharp line across the paper and below it wrote "Challenges" on the chart in big letters and listed four numbers below that. Then he turned to the group and said, "Now I'd like your help telling me what my four challenges will be. If you've been listening to my little talk and descriptions of the difference between me and Dad, you'll have some strong clues. Who wants to go first?" There was about a 20-second pause. Finally Mary raised her hand. Sammy smiled and pointed toward her.

"Maybe you're not as social as your father," she said slowly as if testing each word. People looked her way and then quickly riveted back on Sammy to see how he took the news.

"Yep—I think that's right on the money. Thanks, Mary." And he wrote down "I need help socializing."

"Okay, Mary got us started, who's next?" This time Sammy looked toward George and Vince.

"Maybe you need some help with strategic thinking— you know, big-picture stuff," George said.

Sammy wrote that down—"Strategic thinking."

"Excellent—good stuff. Thanks George. Vince, how about you?"

Vince had kept his eyes down hoping to avoid being called on and then said, "Can I pass on this one?"

"Sure, I shouldn't have put you on the spot. Sorry."

"Anyone else?"

Sean, the young account manager whom Sammy had helped out on his first day jumped in. "Well, by analyzing what you said, I'm guessing that getting help with the emotional side of decision making would help you."

"Great observation. And I appreciate your fast analysis!" People chuckled and were starting to loosen up as Sammy wrote down "Emotional sensitivity" to which Sean nodded approval.

That's when Vince, who had written monthly checks to support Sammy's widely varied ventures when he lived on the West Coast, raised his hand and said, smiling, "I think I speak from experience on this one—you might need just a tad bit of help on focusing." With that George and Mary roared loudest among the others, who also had a good laugh. As he wrote on the chart the final word—

"Focusing" — Sammy smiled and pointed back at Vince as if to say *Okay, you got me.*

So now the chart read:

Sam Williamson

Strengths:

1. Good listener
2. Analytical
3. Logical
4. Good at researching options

Challenges:

1. I need help socializing.
2. Strategic thinking
3. Emotional sensitivity
4. Focusing

"Okay, so my strengths will be what I'll lead with. I'll work on my challenges to do a sort of damage control. I'm never going to be great at these," he said, pointing to his four challenges, "but I promise to work hard at them and will ask you to tell me when I'm hitting the mark or not. Does that sound fair?"

Everyone nodded approval, almost in unison.

"Fair enough, now the last thing. I'd like each of your teams to do the same thing and share your top strengths and challenges with each other. Agreed?"

Again, a chorus of assenting head nods.

Later after Sammy and Mary were back in the executive suite, Sammy asked her, "What did you think?"

She did not look up at first, then took off her glasses and said, "It was interesting."

"But?"

"I'm just not sure how honest people will be. I know I'm hesitant to tell you what I think my challenges are."

"Why?"

"Well, one person's challenge is another person's strength. And besides, I'm not sure it's my job to identify my challenges up front in our working relationship, which might become a barrier and a self-fulfilling prophecy."

"Wow. I'm...I didn't mean it that way. I'm just trying..."

"Sam, I know you're doing what you think is best. I just have a different view of it. And I'm sorry."

Lesson Number Four:
On Change

The next time Sammy came to visit, Uncle Joe sat in his large worn leather chair that provided a crow's-nest overlooking the city. He was sipping his coffee as he watched the sunset illuminate the Empire State Building at "the second most important time of the day," as he described it. Uncle Joe mostly loved the sunrise.

"So, Sammy, how's the company doing?" Uncle Joe asked.

"Pretty good, I'd say."

"That's like telling someone that your sister has pretty hair or your brother has nice eyes."

Sammy smiled but stayed silent.

"Sammy, what's up?"

"Nothing, really. Just a lack of energy."

"Your own lack of energy or others'?"

"Others'."

"Like who?"

"Mary and George."

"So what are they doing or not doing?"

"Nothing, really."

"Maybe that's the problem."

"Yep. It's just that they've all been there so many years. Every time I bring up a new idea or a change, they get all entrenched. I can't seem to unfreeze them to a different way of doing things."

"Teaching old dogs new tricks."

"Yep."

"So let me tell you a story about the shoe repair guy and his kid. We used to have a cobbler—that's what we called the shoe repair guy in the old neighborhood where I grew up," Joe said. "This old Italian guy named Carmelo used to do beautiful hand-tooled leather. So, he was getting along in age and needed help. His kid, Nicholas—Nicky—had been helping the old man in the shop for years—sweeping, cutting, waiting on customers—the usual kind of helper stuff.

"Carmelo starts to teach Nicky how to fix shoes. Nicky's pretty good at it. He's a smart kid and reads a lot. He learns about new automatic machines that make the process faster, better, but his father won't hear of it—not going to happen. Nicky tries, brings in information for his father to read, shows him pictures…tries everything he can to at least be heard. But Carmelo's a stubborn old guy. Eventually, Nicky gets frustrated with the whole thing and joins the army. Then, my god, the tragedy: Nicky gets killed in Vietnam. Carmelo is completely devastated. He eventually goes out of business because he's so depressed, and by now, he can't keep up with the competition's machines—the kind Nicky told him about."

"What a sad story," Sammy said, shaking his head.

"Yep—the exact opposite of what you have."

"Huh?"

"You want the change AND you're the boss—like Carmelo was. Still, change isn't easy even if you're at the top. People resist change, because they're afraid of it. It's fear."

"Fear of what?"

"The unknown. They know what works now. They're comfortable—fat, dumb, and happy. So, you say let's change, and they dig in their heels. It's easier than to change. At least that's what they think."

"So, what should I do?"

"Understand that change takes time and people fear the unknown, so let them have some input. Don't shove it down their throats—or they'll push back harder. Find a good story about change to help them understand. People love stories."

"Okay. I think."

Joe turned to him and pronounced: **"Lesson number four: Change isn't easy, but if you do it right, everyone wins."**

The next day Sammy asked Mary, George, and Vince to have lunch at Sorrento's, an upscale Italian restaurant near the office. He told them he wanted to get out of the office, have some fun, and catch up, and he told them the lunch was his treat!

Paul Sorrento, the middle-aged, portly owner-manager, met them at the door.

"Sammy—great to see you. You're looking more like your father every day." Paul was an old family friend and one of the few people Sam still allowed to call him Sammy.

"You know how to put pressure on a guy, Paul!"

Everyone laughed, because Sam, Sr., had been one of the best-looking men in New York City, especially when he was young.

"So how's business?" Sammy said.

"Booming. Really I'm blessed and lucky," he said winking, knocking on wood, and blessing himself with the sign of the cross. "The new catering business is taking off and the electronic ordering system cuts down on missed orders and confusion, cold meals…the whole bit."

"Good for you."

"Well, enjoy your meal," he said as he seated Sammy and the group and handed out the menus.

"Quite a guy," Sammy said as everyone nodded almost in unison.

The meal went great with talk about movies each had recently seen, new restaurants, and finally about business. George mentioned bringing on a new hire—young woman from Boston; Vince mentioned that the financials looked strong but were leveling off; and Mary talked about the annual dinner dance that the firm was hosting for clients and staff in early fall—right after Labor Day.

Then, Sammy started to speak. "Look, I asked Paul to sit down with us today."

They all looked at each other.

"I want him to tell you the story he told me. After you hear it, I want to chat with you about it. Okay?"

Though they looked a bit surprised, all three nodded and Sammy waved at Paul, who lumbered over to the table and pulled up a chair from the table nearby.

"Paul, I told the team that you would tell them the story you told me about a month ago—about why you changed your business model."

"Sure, Sammy," he said as he waved the waiter to bring him a glass of water. Then he began.

"We were doing well at the restaurant. Sales were up. Everyone was content, all the good signs. My son—Jacob—you know the MBA guy—comes home to visit from Chicago—he tells me the trend in catering is picking up because there are more working parents. He talks to me about automating this and computerizing that. I tell him to look at the books. Don't mess with a good thing, I say. He says, 'Just wait.'

"So, I do. Profits stay steady for a while, and then a few new restaurants crop up down the street. You know—those chain places, and they offer catering. All that. Our bottom line takes one hit and then another hit. I have to start cutting back hours and laying people off. It almost killed me. I love these people like family."

"So my kid calls me from Chicago one night, and I start singing the blues. He reminds me of the catering and the automation. Tells me, at least, to try the catering."

"I give in, hire back a few of the folks part time, set up a catering operation, which we market on our menu and with fliers in the local high-rise office buildings. It's been six months, and already the catering is 20 percent of my gross. And the trend is moving like this," Paul said, drawing an imaginary line in the air with a steep positive incline.

"Really. Twenty percent!" said Vince.

"Not bad, Paul, not bad at all," George said.

"Yeah, then I figure, if the kid's right on this one, I'll try the electronic thing. The ordering system. That was scarier because we had to buy a new system. Cost a boatload, I can tell you. And we had to train the staff. Mamma mia—such a time. Nobody wants to do the new thing. All the waiters and cooks told me it was a lot of bells and whistles, expensive, too much of a hassle.

"We had a sit-down. I picked the three or four waiters and waitresses interested in trying out the system for three months. The cooks had a little more trouble with it, so I worked in the kitchen for the first three weeks, until things were smooth." He paused to take a drink of water.

"So what happened?" Mary asked.

"Well, first I negotiated with the company to get two machines on loan—so it didn't cost us to experiment. They came in and gave my experimental crew training, and we got started. Things were rocky the first week or two, but then got smoother. After a month, the new team was getting out meals much faster and better than the regular crew. The waiters were turning over their tables faster and making more tips. In two months, they were making $25 a night more than their more stubborn buddies. I made them count up their tips every night on top of the bar in plain sight so that everyone could see. I kept track of the speed in the kitchen. The numbers really helped."

"That's a great story, Paul. Thanks for coming by," Sammy said.

"Any time, Sammy."

Sammy pointed at Paul as he walked away and said, **"Change isn't easy, but if you do it right, everyone wins."**

Vince was the first one to speak, "Okay, Sam. I get it."

George and Mary just nodded.

Sammy took out his notebook, opened it, and added lesson four to his growing list:

Lessons Learned

1. No one knows what they're doing until they try.

2. You get what you give. So give a little first.

3. Build trust by character, competence, caring, commitment, and consistency.

4. Change isn't easy, but if you do it right, everyone wins.

Lesson Number Five:
On Vision

Every day when Sammy came to work, he passed a vendor on the street corner in front of his office building. For the first several weeks, Sammy bought a bagel with light cream cheese and a large black coffee and went on his way. After a while, Sammy struck up conversations with the vendor. His name was Ivan. He'd emigrated from Russia and recently gotten his permanent resident alien status—his green card.

One particularly hot August morning, Uncle Joe came into the office with Sammy, as much to take a trip to the other side of town as anything else. So Sammy introduced his Uncle Joe to Ivan, and as always when he met someone for the first time, Joe acted like he and Ivan had been friends for years.

"So Ivan, how long you been on the corner?"

"Almost six year now."

"So how's business?"

"Good. Gets slow in the summer."

"Vacations you think?"

"Yes. I think."

"How'd you pick this spot to set up on?"

"The man, who owned this stand before me, says this was good place. So, I stay here."

"I see," Uncle Joe said looking around the area.

"You ever try a different corner to see if it's better?"

"Just one time."

"When?"

"A few months ago, they do construction here on this sidewalk. They tell me I must move then for couple weeks."

"Where'd you go?"

"Across the street, there," he said pointing to a shaded spot shrouded by a couple of huge trees.

"Looks like a shaded, cool location," Joe said.

"Much cooler."

"What happened to your sales?"

"They went up, especially in the afternoon."

"How much?"

"Maybe 15 percent higher—could be 20 percent."

"That's pretty damned good! Then what happened?"

"When they finish construction, I go back to my old spot."

"So, you never tried that spot again?"

"No. I get used to this spot, I guess."

Looking at a line forming behind them, Sammy said, "Uncle Joe, there are other people who need caffeine. Let's get going."

"My nephew—always in a rush, this kid. Well, it's nice to meet you, Ivan. I'm looking at the shade over there," he pointed to the place Ivan had moved temporarily, "and I'm thinking that in the summer, with all the shade, it might be a better place for your business. Anyway, see you later."

"Thank you."

The next day when Sammy came to work, Ivan was set up on the other side of the street under the spreading maple trees.

"Morning, Ivan."

"Hey, Sam."

"You moved?"

"Yes, I got the idea from your uncle."

"Hope it works out for you."

"So far, so good. I keep track," he said, showing Sammy a notebook and pencil.

After a few months, the weather started to turn cold, but Ivan stayed under the trees until one day Joe came back with Sammy to the office.

"Joe. Good seeing you."

"You too, Ivan."

"How's your business doing?"

"Good, but..."

"What."

"My business slipped off—was great last few months. Then went down."

"You ever think of going back to your old spot over there where it's sunnier?"

"No, it work good, so I stay here."

"Maybe it's the shade. Great in summer but not so great in the winter."

Ivan hit his head, "Yes. I see. I'll give a try tomorrow."

On the way to the office, Sammy turned to Joe. "You're something else, Uncle Joe."

"How's that?"

"You helped Ivan without blinking an eye."

"I help anyone—especially people I like. Taking a hard look at something that's been working for a long time is difficult. You get used to parking your car in a certain spot, you get used to eating at a certain restaurant or going to a particular grocery store. That becomes your default. Most times, we never question what works—even if it changes—especially if it changes gradually."

"I guess you're right. It's easy to get into a groove, even seductive."

"A fancy way of putting it...but yeah...seductive," Joe said, winking. "I like to think of it as the V-Thing."

"What?"

"The vision thing. If you can stop yourself every now and then and check all your basic assumptions, you may find you've been doing things a certain way—and those things could certainly stand a re-Vision."

That afternoon at their regular senior executive meeting, Sammy leaned back and asked George and Vince, "What are some of the basic assumptions we're operating on at the company?"

"What?" George said with his usual twisted-face look when someone asked him a question he didn't really understand. Vince nodded in tortured agreement but remained silent.

"I mean...take for example, how long have we been in this building?"

"Maybe 20 years, since it was built. Why?" George asked.

"We ever look around for new space. Cheaper? Better? Closer to where our employees live now?"

"No. Not really. Nobody ever asked."

"Maybe we should have."

"Why?"

"Let me ask you another question."

George winced slightly, but nodded and said, "Yes."

"Why did you pick this place?"

"Actually, your father picked it."

"Why?"

George turned to Vince as he wrinkled his forehead, looking for help from the still-quiet Vince.

"It was the most modern place around at the time and had good surface parking next to the building," George finally said.

"Surface parking, you mean where the new Comstock building is now?"

"Yes," said George.

"How do most people get to work these days?"

"The executives drive and park in the building."

"But what about the rest of the employees? Especially the lower-paid folks."

"They have to take the train and the bus to get here."

"How expensive is that?"

George looked at Vince and nodded. "I see where you're going with this."

"George, let me ask you a favor. Please get a group of employees together and ask them what they think their vision of an ideal place to work would look like. I'm talking now about the building. What facilities would it have—lobby, gym, parking? Where would it be located for the best commuting? Those kinds of questions."

"Are you sure? You'll open up a big can of worms."

"Yeah, but it might help our fishing. Let's try it."

"Okay, if you say so," George said—but you could almost hear his heels digging into the carpet.

That evening at one of his regular dinners with Uncle Joe, Sammy told him what he'd done about questioning the location of the office and how he'd tasked George with finding answers—re-Visioning the whole deal. Suddenly, Joe got very quiet.

"What is it, Uncle Joe? I thought you'd be happy."

Joe cleared his throat and wiped his eyes.

"What's wrong? You okay?" Sammy asked as he became more concerned.

Joe waved him off, "Sure, I'm fine. It's just that...."

"What?"

"Well maybe 30 some years ago, your father and I had this same sort of conversation about where to put the office. I asked him what his vision for the office was."

"Really? What did he say?"

"He saw a place where people came to work refreshed and ready to contribute. He saw a clean, professional place easy to get to, near places to eat, and among the businesses that would become his clients."

"So where did he start?"

"Same place you did—asking the employees their vision for a great workplace. He trusted people, and in turn, they trusted Sam back."

"So, is this another lesson I'm getting without knowing what to call it?"

"You got it. Remember in the Broadway musical *South Pacific* when the old woman sings, 'If you don't have a dream, how you gonna make that dream come true?'"

"Oh, yeah."

"Sammy, **Lesson number five: You have to have a vision to make it come true.**"

Sammy pulled out his notebook and updated it.

Lessons Learned

1. No one knows what they're doing until they try.

2. You get what you give. So give a little first.

3. Build trust by character, competence, caring, commitment, and consistency.

4. Change isn't easy, but if you do it right, everyone wins.

5. You have to have a vision to make it come true.

Lesson Number Six: On Creating a Positive Culture

Every day when Sammy came into the office, he passed through the lobby where the corporate logo hung, and next to it was the mission statement: "To provide the best consulting advice to our client-partners. Our Values: Respect, Integrity, and Innovation."

Today, when he got into his office, he asked Mary, "Do you know what the company mission statement is?"

She looked at him with a curious look, then an embarrassed glance, and said, "Something about helping clients?"

"Close. How about the company values?"

"What?"

"Our company values."

"Yeah…," she said, then paused. "Respect?" She paused again, and then said, "I guess not really."

"Thanks. Is George in?"

Within ten minutes, Sammy was in George's office, asking him the same questions he'd asked Mary.

"Sammy, I mean, Sam," he stuttered, "I'm ashamed I couldn't tell you exactly. The mission statement and values thing was your dad's idea. He was big on it." George paused. "I wasn't."

"Why?"

"I'm not one for all the leadership hocus-pocus stuff."

"You think that's what a mission statement is—hocus-pocus?"

"I'm into executing—getting things done—not thinking about it or writing a fancy statement on a wall."

"What things do you get done?"

"Sammy, this is stupid."

"I disagree, George. Getting things done is great if they're the right things to get done."

"Look, I have a meeting I'm already late for," George said, getting up and walking toward the door.

"We'll talk about this later, George, because...."

George walked out before Sammy could finish his sentence.

The following Saturday afternoon, Sammy and Uncle Joe were taking Joe's weekly walk through Central Park. There were hundreds of people on in-line skates, running, biking, sunbathing, walking dogs, playing softball, and strolling—like Joe and Sammy.

Sammy turned and said to Joe, "George told me that Dad was big into mission statements and corporate values."

"Not at first."

"Really?"

"Your father was smart...sometimes too smart."

"Too smart?"

"Sam had such a fast mind that he lost people quickly. And the man had zero degrees of patience—none, nada. To say he did not suffer fools lightly is, uh, was, a gross understatement."

"I see."

"He was impatient and wanted to build the company too fast—on his own. I hate to say it, but your father could be an intellectual bully."

"A bully?"

"His speed. His big brain left a lot of people in the dust. And he didn't wait for them. As a result, his business started to lose people."

"People quit?"

"Exactly. That's what they do if they don't feel appreciated, respected, and valued for what they bring to the table. And if they can't fight back because you're the boss, they vote with their feet."

"Ah, I see."

"So one day, we're having lunch, and Sam asks me why he's losing so many people. I tell him because he's acting like a jerk."

Sammy roared so hard that he had to stop walking for a minute. People running by looked at him as if he might be choking, but he waved them off.

Joe continued his story. "I ask him if he wants more of my opinion. 'Yes,' he says. So I tell him to ask people what they think the company should do, what they should believe in — real values and beliefs. That's what motivates people."

"And that's how the mission and values came to be — the ones that hang in the lobby?"

"Yes. Problem is that it's only part of the formula for a successful culture."

"Culture?"

"Yeah, culture's the atmosphere that people breathe inside a company. If it's clean and fresh, the company is healthy. But if it's stale — or worse, polluted — the company's in trouble — choking."

"Clean and fresh?"

"Yes. If ideas are bubbling up from people at every level, especially those charged with the responsibility for executing them — then the air is fresh. If people are not afraid to disagree — it's fresh. If people can try, fail, learn, and try again — then, the atmosphere is fresh."

"Then, I think the company's stale, not polluted, yet," Sammy said. "But certainly a long way from fresh."

"I agree, and the distance between stale and polluted can narrow quickly."

"So how do you turn it around?"

"Do a culture inventory."

"What?"

"Start back with the people. Ask them what the unwritten rules are."

"Unwritten rules?"

"People believe what they see, not what they're told. Let me give you an example. If a father tells his teenaged son not to drink and drive, but that kid sees his father come home tipsy after stopping for a few drinks himself, what do you think that kid thinks the real family rule is about drinking and driving?"

"So if there's a conflict, go with what people do, not just what they say."

"Yep, Sammy, **Lesson number six: If you want to create a positive culture, show people by your actions what you believe in, don't just tell them.**"

"I see."

"And Sammy, if the culture's toxic, nothing—no matter how good—will grow. On the other hand, if it's fresh, everything will thrive."

The next day Sammy called an all-company meeting. Before the meeting, George and Vince came into his office to get the scoop, but Sammy said he wanted to talk to everyone at the same time. George was particularly insistent—bordering on rude—but Sammy told him to hold on.

Only 50 of the 75 employees showed up at the meeting. Others would hear about it within minutes after the meeting, Sammy figured, so he wasn't too concerned.

When they were all settled in the largest conference room in the building, Sammy stepped up to the microphone and said, "Thanks for coming. I've asked Mary to give each of you five index cards."

Mary was moving throughout the crowd passing out the cards.

"I want to do a little exercise—a completely anonymous one. I'm looking for truth—not bull—okay?"

People nodded cautiously as they awaited the instructions.

"On the first card, I want you to list as many company *unwritten rules* as you can think of," Sammy said. He then paused and repeated it for emphasis. "The unwritten, even unspoken, rules that you learned early on when you came to work for the company. I'm not looking for feel-good stuff. I want the truth. So, I'd like you to print your answers on one card. Something like, 'I learned that to get anything done, I had to kiss up to my supervisor.'"

A number of the staff laughed out loud; some chuckled and winked at each other.

"Or, 'I found early that I could not bring bad news to my boss because he always shot the messenger.' That's what I'm looking for. So take a few minutes and label the first card '1.' When you're finished, Mary will pick up the cards and give them directly to me—NO ONE ELSE. And since I don't know everyone's handwriting much less printing, I'll be objective in reviewing them."

After five minutes of watching people think and then print intently, Sammy stepped back up to the podium and said, "Label the next card '2.' On this card, write down the values and beliefs of the company. Not the ones you may have been told, but values that we enforce and or reinforce by what we *do* every day. As an example, you might print

'We value getting to work on time,' or 'We believe you have to be at your desk to be productive,' or 'We don't work a minute after 5:00 at night,' or 'Clients are a real pain.' Again, I want you to be honest, as brutal as that might be."

After five minutes, Sammy came back up to the podium and said, "Okay, on card '3,' what are our traditions and stories? List them—the good, the bad, and the ugly. Write what you believe is true: Like, 'We always reward the smilers' or 'We skip out of work early on Fridays' or 'We fudge our time on our client's time cards.' Again—honesty is always better than a bunch of baloney."

He waited as people wrote. In a few minutes, Mary picked up the cards, and like she had done with cards labeled "1" and "2," she brought this set of cards directly to Sammy at the podium, where he turned them upside down, like the other two sets.

"On card '4,' paint your own picture of the ideal way our company should look. How would you like the company to work? What would you and your colleagues be doing if the company were doing things exceptionally well? Maybe 'I'd be having open and frank conversations with my supervisor about problems with my client,' or 'I'd tell the client when I don't think our company can be of maximum value to him or her.'"

Then Sammy said after a few minutes of writing, "Fine, now on the final card, number '5,' tell me what I didn't ask you. Tell me anything you think I should know. Again, honesty helps me the most."

After Mary collected the five cards and gave them to Sammy, he held them high to show the thick stack to the assembled group. Then lifting the cards up, he said, "Thank you for your hard work today. I will read these, analyze them, and get back to you in one week with the results of what you told me anonymously. And if you've been honest, I'm sure that patterns will emerge that will help us chart a new course at the company. I will not only listen to you — I will absolutely listen to everything you tell me. Thank you all for taking this time to help the company."

Then Sammy stepped away from the microphone. Dead silence...until he got near the door to leave. The applause started from the back of the room, where the techies had huddled, and then it moved forward like a wave. Sammy felt a surge of electricity run up his spine, toward his tear ducts. So he stuck up his right arm as he headed toward the door with dispatch. He again thought about what Joe had told him: **Lesson Number Six: If you want to create a positive culture, show people by your actions what you believe in, don't just tell them.**

When he got back to his office, he added it to his notebook.

Lessons Learned

1. No one knows what they're doing until they try.

2. You get what you give. So give a little first.

3. Build trust by character, competence, caring, commitment, and consistency.

4. Change isn't easy, but if you do it right, everyone wins.

5. You have to have a vision to make it come true.

6. If you want to create a positive culture, show people by your actions what you believe in, don't just tell them.

Lesson Number Seven:
On Courage

After Sammy wrote in his notebook, he stared at the thick stack of index cards on his desk. Mary was the first one to come in. She moved toward his desk and reached to take the cards, saying, "Sam, I'll take those and type them up for you and have them all done by tomorrow morning."

Sammy gently put his hand on the stack. "No thanks, Mary. I'd like to do them myself."

She reached again, saying, "I can have them done…"

"No thanks," he interrupted, and moved them a few inches away from her grasp. "I appreciate the offer, really. Thank you."

Mary stiffened and backed away. "Fine."

About five minutes later, George blustered in and closed the door behind him. "Sammy… Sam, what the hell are you doing?"

Sammy, who was already sorting cards into five neat stacks looked up and asked, "What?"

"Are you trying to stir up the natives?"

"Who?"

"Are you trying to start an insurrection?"

"Natives? Insurrection? George, what are you talking about?"

"You keep doing these touchy-feely exercises, and you'll have the nuts running the nuthouse." By now George was red in the face. "Now let me see those cards, and let me do my job running this company," he said. "I'll handle everything."

"Whoa, George. Take a deep breath."

"Deep breath? I've been taking deep breaths since you…"

"George, I think before you go any further, you need to take a time out, and we'll talk later."

"A time out. I'm not some four-year-old kid, Sam. A damned time out!"

Sammy got up from his desk, came around the front of it, walked George to the door, and said, "I'll come by and see you later."

George stared at Sammy with pinpoint pupils that would have spit if they could have. He pivoted and left the office. Sam closed the door, took a deep breath, and then went back to his cards. He stayed sequestered in his office until almost 8:00 that night, long after everyone had gone home, including Mary, who had stayed an extra hour, and finally tried one more time to get the cards from Sammy before she left for the evening.

The cards began to tell five interesting and related stories.

Stack one—the unwritten rules—had statements, which in one form or another kept being repeated and reinforced:

- "It's not what you know, but who you know that gets you promoted."
- "Don't work too hard, or other people might not look so good and resent it."
- "Clients are our meal tickets."
- "Mary rules the roost."
- "George really runs the place, not the CEO."
- "Don't bring bad news forward, or you will get shot."
- "Don't make waves."

- "Don't show any vulnerability, or you'll be seen as weak."
- "George is vindictive. Be careful of him."

Stack two—the *real* values and beliefs of the company—also had some repeated themes:

- "Integrity"
- "Hard work"
- "Revenue is king."
- "People come last—work comes first."
- "If you work hard, you get paid. That's your only reward."
- "Just do your job."
- "Independence"
- "Accountability"
- "Your paycheck IS your only praise."

Stack three—traditions and stories—was the smallest deck, but in some ways the most interesting:

- "The company softball team really is the place to get politically connected—George is the coach."
- "When the company was founded, Sam had a clear vision, but something happened along the way."
- "Everyone is expected to come to the holiday party with a spouse or significant other regardless of their holiday travel plans."

Stack four—paint the ideal picture of the company—came next, and like the previous three stacks, this one also opened Sammy's eyes. The ideal picture they painted implied that it did not now exist, which captured Sammy's undivided attention:

- "A fun place where people laugh more"
- "People working together on teams"
- "No back stabbing — but back patting"
- "Less of a prison mentality"
- "Everyone rowing the boat in the same direction"
- "Respect for the opinions of others"
- "Value diversity in opinion, gender, and race"
- "A place free from retaliation"

Stack five — what else should I know — capped the effort.

- "This isn't a bad place, but it could be a LOT better."
- "I wouldn't want to be in your [Sam's] shoes."
- "Is your head really in this game, or are you just checking it out, marking time?"
- "I'm not sure I trust you — yet."
- "Be very careful of George."
- "Good luck."

The last one got to Sammy — "Good luck." Yes, he thought, he'd need more than a little good luck. With that, he gathered up all the cards — every single one — banded them in stacks, stuck them in his briefcase, and called Joe.

When Sammy arrived at Joe's apartment, Joe was tinkering with a model car on his kitchen table, which was covered with newspaper. He had a large collection of antique cars, which he had assembled over the years with glue and his trusty toothpicks. Sammy sat down after letting himself in—Joe only locked the door when he went to bed.

"So, Mr. CEO, how are you tonight?" Joe asked as he glued a rear quarter panel on a black Model T Ford.

"Tired. Long day."

"I can see."

"I did what you suggested."

"Sammy, I'm old. You gotta be more specific."

"I asked the people what they thought—the unwritten rules."

"Ah, yes. The truth."

"Exactly. I also asked them a few other questions about values, traditions, what the ideal company would look like, and what else I should know."

"So what did you learn?"

"Several things—first, there's a lack of trust inside the company. People are afraid to excel, to stick their necks out—that sort of thing. Second, they don't feel valued or like they matter one way or the other. Third, revenue is what it's all about. Finally, George is a BIG problem."

Then Sammy read the detailed lists under the five different headings to Joe, who listened, glued, and chuckled at certain points during Sammy's recitation.

"Hmm. I'd say that you asked the people for the truth, and they told it to you."

"So why didn't you tell me about George?"

"Remember the show-don't-tell rule?"

Sammy nodded, realizing that if he had not done the research himself but had only listened to what Joe told him, it would never have been as powerful a lesson.

After considering the subtle but critical lesson Joe had just taught him, Sammy asked, "So now what do I do?"

"What did you tell the employees that you'd do with the cards after you reviewed them?"

"That I'd report back to them in one week about what I found."

"Sounds like a good plan to me."

"But, what about George?"

"Tell the truth about what they said about you—be brutally honest. And tell what they said about George—maybe not so brutally honest—but honest. But make sure you tell George what you'll be doing before you do it. He will be mad but will, at least, respect you for the heads up."

"But I'm not sure I can be THAT honest."

"You don't have a choice if you want to become the leader."

"I'm not sure I do."

With that, Joe put down the toothpick with the tiny glistening dab of glue on the end of it, and he took off his glasses. He turned squarely toward Sammy and said, "Sammy, **Lesson number seven: Leadership is all about courage.**"

Sammy just stared at Uncle Joe.

"If you don't want to be a leader, step down. But if you do want to lead, you have to *step up*...and call hard shots. Tell the truth when it's not comfortable. That's what leaders do."

"But I'm just not sure about my findings."

"Baloney. You know George is a problem. In fact, George knows he's a problem, and I guarantee he's heard this information before."

"How so?"

"Because your father told him the same thing. But..."

"But what?"

"Look, Sammy. God rest your father's soul, but he didn't have the heart to discipline George, his longest and dearest friend. In the end, he hung on to George too long, and it hurt the business."

"Hurt the business?"

"George cost the company a number of great employees and a fair share of customers with his my-way-or-the-highway attitude."

Sammy nodded slowly, paused for a while, pulled out his notebook, and added Lesson Number Seven to his list.

Lessons Learned

1. No one knows what they're doing until they try.

2. You get what you give. So give a little first.

3. Build trust by character, competence, caring, commitment, and consistency.

4. Change isn't easy, but if you do it right, everyone wins.

5. You have to have a vision to make it come true.

6. If you want to create a positive culture, show people by your actions what you believe in, don't just tell them.

7. Leadership is all about courage.

Lesson Number Eight:
On Taking a First Bold Step

That weekend, Sammy worked on the staff survey report that he had promised. It wasn't that the report was so long; it was that he spent a good deal of time trying to soften the findings about George.

In the end, he decided to do as Joe had suggested — to tell the truth. To do the least amount of ego damage, he had picked Friday afternoon to release the report. It was difficult for him to wait until then, but he believed it would be easiest on George this way, so he waited.

On Friday mid-afternoon he called Mary into his office. She had been cool toward him all week ever since he refused to let her process the survey cards herself. Now, she sat in front of his desk as he spoke, "Mary, you know I've been working on the results of the survey I took at the all-company meeting a week ago."

She nodded, still trying to retain a pleasant smile.

"I've been working on the report pretty hard."

She nodded.

"I'm finished and will release the report this after-noon."

Again she smiled and nodded.

"People made some tough remarks about me: that they were not sure if I was really serious about running the company, that I was not as committed as my father, that I was not experienced… that sort of stuff."

She nodded with her head cocked to one side as if to say *There, there, it's all right, Sammy.*

"I had to be honest, so I put that all in the report. I was a little uncomfortable but thought I should tell the truth. What do you think about that?"

She paused and said, "I think it's always best to tell the truth."

"Good. Thanks, I thought you might say that. So I've decided to be honest and true to the data I collected from that meeting."

Again, she nodded this time with a more engaged smile.

"There were also a few comments about you and George by name."

She fixed her look on Sammy and sat up taller and asked, "Such as?"

"I have to be honest with you — like the comments they made about me, their comments about George and you were painfully honest."

"Me?" she asked with emphasis.

Sammy cleared his throat and spoke softly, "I'll just read the quote: 'Mary rules the roost.'"

She smiled. "Well, everyone knows I do try to protect your time and availability. So, I confess. Guilty as charged."

"We'll need to work on that perception, Mary. I wouldn't like it if I thought people were intimidated about coming in to see me."

"But your father," she started to say.

"Dad and I are very different."

"Of course."

"Look, I know you're only trying to protect me, and I appreciate that. But I want people — everyone at the company — to feel like they have access to me — especially on a one-on-one, confidential basis. Okay?"

"Sure. You'll just have to remind me — for a while."

"Will do. Now, would you ask George to come in?"

"Sure," she said and left the office.

When George came into the office, Sammy got up and ushered him to the conversation area where the couch and leather chairs were, near the rear of his office. He explained the criticism about himself that he'd be putting into the report.

"Are you nuts?" George said with a puzzled look on his face.

"Why do you say that?"

"Publishing your weaknesses? That's corporate suicide."

"But I also think it's the honest thing to do."

"Honest? It's crazy. I strongly advise you against it."

"I'm staying true to my word."

"I wouldn't."

"Well, then I have some more tough news."

"Like what?"

"Several references were made about you that I'll be including in the report."

"Like what?"

"I'm quoting here, 'George really runs the place, not the CEO,'" he said, reading the text directly from the stapled report.

"Well, as the COO, I do run the day-to-day operations of the company. It's not that far off. But drop it from the report."

"No, I don't want to edit out anything that showed up repeatedly, and that did."

"Your call, Sam, but I wouldn't do it."

"There's another quote I'm going to use."

"Shoot."

"George is vindictive—be careful."

"Who said that?"

At first Sammy just looked at him, but then said, "This quote or one like it surfaced no less than four times—and they are anonymous, if you recall."

"No way you should use such a quote."

"I intend to."

George stood up and towered over Sammy saying, "Sam, this is nuts. And, I find it personally offensive. I can't warn you more strongly. DON'T do this." As he spoke, George's face turned beet red.

"I don't think I'd be authentic if I didn't."

"Authentic?" he said with a raised voice and with his hands on his hips.

"If you prefer—*honest* instead of *authentic*."

"This is ridiculous. We...I...your father," he said, and then finally exploded. "If you do this, I'll quit."

"I would hate to lose you, George, but this report will go out after you and I finish this conversation."

"We're finished SAMMY...you little.... What made you think you could come in here and run a company. You don't know squat, you sanctimonious little...I QUIT," George roared.

Sammy didn't say anything. As George stormed out, Sammy heard him bark something to Mary, and she left right after him.

That afternoon around 2:00 p.m., Sammy hit the "send" button on his e-mail, and within seconds, all of his employees had the report, which warned that no one should share the report outside the "Williamson family," as a matter of trust. Within the hour, those who were in the office were buzzing among themselves with an energy that Sammy hadn't seen since he had come to the company nearly three months ago. And he received his first e-mail from the most unlikely source, Ralph, a longtime blue-collar employee, who worked in the mailroom and supplies.

"Thanks for being a straight shooter," was all it said, but it spoke volumes to Sammy.

By the time he left later that evening, he had received five other e-mails, some more elegant than Ralph's, but none more meaningful to Sammy. He felt as if a weight were lifted from him. He called Joe and asked to meet him for a bite at the deli.

Eddie greeted Sammy as usual when he approached the booth where Joe was sitting and already chewing a piece of bread. "What took you so long? I was starving," Joe said, wiping the crumbs away.

"A couple of people stopped me on the way out of work to talk about the report. Here, look it over while I hit the men's room," Sammy said. He slid the seven-page report toward Joe, who eagerly devoured it almost as energetically as he did the bread.

About five minutes later, Sammy returned to the table and was about to say something, when Joe raised his hand for silence. And after he finished the report he put it down and said, "So, you sent this out?"

"Yes." He paused. "George quit."

"I'm not surprised. Good riddance."

"What! I thought you'd be shocked."

"More happy than shocked. Look, he's been a sour apple in that company for the past 15 years. And, your father, God bless him, placed a lot of value in loyalty. I told him to move out George a long time ago. He just couldn't do it. So, good for you, Sammy."

"I'm not sure about Mary either."

"I wouldn't worry about her. If she goes, not to worry."

"Well, why didn't you tell me this beforehand?"

"Remember the show-don't-tell rule. I tell you, and you think I'm either a genius or a nut...more likely a nut. So, you're feeling pretty good right now?"

"Yes, I am."

"Good, enjoy it for a few minutes."

"What?"

"Now the really heavy lifting begins."

"What?"

"Making changes. Going from what is to what you want it to be."

"I see."

"The first three questions you asked tell you where you are—a place where people don't trust each other, there's fear, and the power is in the hands of a few people, who can be nasty."

Sammy pulled the report back from Joe and went to the pages that analyzed the results of the card survey and said, "Yes, essentially."

"The fourth question tells you where they want to be— in a place where people work together on a common goal, are respected for what they do and their opinions, and where people trust one another. Not too complicated, but difficult to actually do."

"So, how do I do it?"

"We'll talk more this weekend. For now you've learned **Lesson number eight: The long march begins with the first bold step.** Now eat—your soup is getting cold."

Again, Sammy took out his small notebook and added to his growing list.

Lessons Learned

1. No one knows what they're doing until they try.

2. You get what you give. So give a little first.

3. Build trust by character, competence, caring, commitment, and consistency.

4. Change isn't easy, but if you do it right, everyone wins.

5. You have to have a vision to make it come true.

6. If you want to create a positive culture, show people by your actions what you believe in, don't just tell them.

7. Leadership is all about courage.

8. The long march begins with the first bold step.

Lesson Number Nine:
On Staying Grounded

On Monday morning when people started to arrive at Williamson Associates, Sammy was already in and working hard. In fact, he'd been working there much of the weekend and had e-mailed the staff that he wanted to meet again in the large conference room at 10:00 a.m.

The entire office was buzzing over George's resignation. So Sammy was feeling a little strong yet very weak at this particular moment. Indirectly, he'd made a bold change—but now what? The first person he called in before the staff meeting was Vince.

"Vince, you know that George quit."

"Yes," Vince said.

"How does that make you feel?"

"Surprised."

"I understand that. I just want you to know that I hope you stay with me...the company."

"Okay," Vince said, not really looking at Sammy.

"Really, I mean it. You're experienced and know the business."

"So did George," Vince said, this time looking right into Sammy's eyes.

"I know, but you saw the report."

"Yeah, I saw the report."

"You sound like you disagree with it."

"No. I disagree with sending it out to everyone."

"I can appreciate that. But I promised to be honest and was."

"Yeah."

"But you don't agree."

"Right."

"Fair enough, for now. I just ask that you stay with me for three months. Then if you're still not convinced I'm for real, we'll figure out an alternative."

"I'll think about it."

"Okay, thanks."

The staff meeting started promptly at 10:00 a.m. When Sammy entered the room, the roar of conversation stilled. Sammy looked around and said, "Boy, I sure can kill a party!" Everyone laughed.

"So, let's get started." He paused and looked around the room. "Nobody likes change. I'd put myself at the head of that line. Mostly, nobody likes to BE changed."

A few people snickered as Sammy began. "You all know I lived in California, leading a pretty nice life in Carmel-by-the-Sea. When my dad died, I had no idea he'd ask me to run this company. Frankly, that was the kind of change I didn't ask for or want," Sammy said, as he pulled up the blank sheet of flip chart paper exposing the first page.

Sam's Life Changes

Was Then	Is Now
Chilling out	Working hard
Carmel	NYC
No responsibility	CEO
Easy	Hard
Old, familiar	New, different
Content	Uncertain

"My life has changed radically in the past several months. I was living carefree on the West Coast with no responsibility other than working out and hanging out with my friends. I went from the familiar place where I'd gone to school and hung out, to New York City, to becoming a CEO in an unfamiliar setting. To be honest, I was shell-shocked."

People nodded; a few laughed.

"But with the help from people like Vince, Mary, and George—and my Uncle Joe, whom most of you know at least in passing—I've learned a lot in the past three months. But I learned as much from you just this weekend." He flipped the page.

Survey Findings

1. People are afraid to excel—to stick their necks out/take chances. There are trust issues.

2. People don't feel valued or that they matter.

3. Revenue is what it's all about.

4. George is a problem.

Even though the staff had already seen these findings in the report, seeing them in bold print in such a public setting was so stark and candid as to be embarrassing. Sammy stood back and said, "Look, culture in any organization takes years to develop. For a lot of very good reasons, this firm—under my father's leadership and that of George, Vince, and others—has prospered. There's no denying that. In the meantime, the world has changed. In fact, every second we're alive, we're changing. It's small and incremental, but we're changing. The trick is to move with the change and focus on a positive target."

At that point, an employee in the back of the room blurted out, "Why did you fire George?"

"The short answer is—I didn't. George quit." Sammy paused to collect his thoughts. "Look, I'm not happy about what happened. But I promised everyone I'd tell the truth, no matter what. And I did. Honestly, I thought about ways around doing that, but decided that my word to you all was more important than my personal comfort. So, we need to deal with these findings—trust, being valued, revenue, and problems with certain people. I don't intend on solving them today, but I selected employee names at random from an alphabetical roster and am appointing four working teams. The teams will begin to address the most important issues raised in the report. I'll give out the team lists when I finish. If you do not want to participate, I'll pick someone else. I hope that's clear."

Just then Vince spoke. "I've got something to say."

Sammy held his breath. He worried about what Vince might say, especially considering his current frame of mind.

"When Sammy—excuse me, Sam—came into the office the first day, I thought the whole idea of his taking over as CEO was nuts."

People laughed, then quickly sobered once they realized that Sammy had a somber look on his face, and stared at Vince.

"But then I saw Sam do things…take some actions that frankly I think we should've done about ten years ago. He's right about change. Just look at me."

People chuckled.

"We've stayed in the same groove we've been in for years. Our sales are flat and our strategic plan, such as it is...well, it's pretty uninspiring. I hate to say that because I wrote it."

Another collective chuckle from the gallery.

"Change is about loss. It's like a death. You give up something familiar, dependable for something unknown, unproven."

Everyone in the room went silent because they knew this was personal for Vince.

"Most of you know that Rachel, my wife, died two years ago. That was the toughest time in my life. At first I was shocked, then I denied it, then I got angry at her for leaving me, angry at God for taking her, and even angry at myself for not being able to do something."

He cleared his throat for a second or two, while people waited for what came next.

"Finally, I got very sad — I was depressed. But after a year or so, I began to focus on the future — to accept what had happened and move on, but not forget. Never."

Again he took a deep breath and cleared his throat.

"The changes at Williamson have been happening for years. In fact, change is inevitable. The difference is that Sammy — Sam, I mean — is ALLOWING you to determine the change yourselves. For some people, this will be tougher than others. I'm sorry George quit, but maybe it was best for him. I don't know. But I'm sticking around to see this transition through. I'm not saying I'll be here forever — I'm way too old for that. But Sam's making sense. So here's my message — my lesson for you all: **Change will happen — embrace it while sticking to your core principles**," he said, and paused.

Then he said, "I especially suggest you stick to the single principle that makes this company great—the one that Sam's dad started this company with: Keep the client first."

Slowly, as Vince remained standing, people started to clap and stand up. And Sammy took out his notepad and added Vince's lesson to his list.

Lessons Learned

1. No one knows what they're doing until they try.

2. You get what you give. So give a little first.

3. Build trust by character, competence, caring, commitment, and consistency.

4. Change isn't easy, but if you do it right, everyone wins.

5. You have to have a vision to make it come true.

6. If you want to create a positive culture, show people by your actions what you believe in, don't just tell them.

7. Leadership is all about courage.

8. The long march begins with the first bold step.

9. Change will happen—embrace it while sticking to your core principles.

Lesson Number Ten:
On People

The next few months for Sammy were like boot camp in the Marine Corps: he slept fewer hours, got up before sunrise, got into the office before anyone, and left after most everyone as he dealt with some corporate whining, straightened out a few business and personnel messes, and managed many changes. Some people quit and moved on to other companies, clients adjusted to the new company that Sammy had shaped, and Williamson Associates embraced a new economy that involved more active use of the Internet than the company had been used to. But under Sammy's leadership, the company practiced its core principle: keep the client first.

Lots of good things happened to Sammy. Vince became Sammy's strongest ally, and Mary got used to Sammy's open-door policy, even if it rubbed her raw some days.

That year, the company actually expanded its revenue by 10 percent after a very rocky start—when the old-timers had pressured Sammy to go back to the way things were. He had stayed the course and held tight. Now he was starting to look smarter by the week. His mother had started traveling again and seemed to emerge from her dark cloud of grief. However, Uncle Joe had gotten sick and had to be placed in a nursing home on Long Island—"the woods," Joe had often called it. Everyone in the neighborhood thought of it as someplace so un–New York. Sammy not only visited Joe every weekend and holiday but also paid for his care, which Joe never realized.

On a bright Saturday, Sammy walked into Uncle Joe's room. Joe was sitting in a wheelchair that faced the woods behind the facility. In his striped bathrobe, his legs covered by a white cotton blanket, he was reading intently, as he so often did. With a new book of his own under his arm and a cup of coffee, Sammy went over and kissed his uncle on the crown of his head.

Pleasantly startled, Joe turned his head, took off his bifocals, and said, "Well, it's my nephew, the entrepreneur."

"You're looking well, Uncle Joe."

"Sure. Still chasing the old ladies with my walker!"

"Be careful. You might just catch one," Sammy said, wagging his finger at Joe.

"God forbid."

"What are you reading?"

"Another novel about lawyers and doctors. I'm wondering, does no one else have an interesting life? Always it's the lawyers and the doctors," Joe said.

"Strange," said Sammy, "The lawyers and doctors I know don't lead very interesting lives."

Joe laughed, nodded, and said, "So how are you, Mr. CEO?"

"I'm well. The usual ups and downs but more ups than downs these days."

"And Vince?"

"He's actually dating!"

"What?"

"He's seeing a lady friend. He met a wealthy widow on a cruise to Europe, and they've been seeing each other for six months now."

"Good for him. And your mother visits me regularly...she looks good."

"Yes the travel agrees with her, too. She goes with her sidekick, Edna."

"Tell me about the company."

"Not much I haven't told you already. Overall, we're doing well. At least the suggestions from the staff keep coming in, our turnover rate has slowed to a drip, and our new client base grows weekly. Best of all we're holding most of our old clients, and our revenues are up."

"How about that grumpy client...Mr. Bolton?"

"Aching Al Bolton! He's still with us, crotchety as ever, but we've managed to keep him on. Every now and then I have to go smooth his ruffled feathers."

"I guess he's worth it to you."

"Not sure, but he's a challenge and keeps me grounded."

"How about Mary?"

"She's let up on the reins a bit. Still has trouble, but she's working on it. She's loyal. Glad she's trying."

"I'm glad, too. She's valuable and as loyal as the day is long."

"I agree," Sammy said, finally sitting in the chair next to Joe's wheelchair.

Joe closed his book, turned to Sammy, and said, "So, it's been a year. You did it."

"Did it?"

"As of last Monday, it's been a year you've been running the company."

"Wow, that's right. I actually lost track of the date!"

"That's a good sign."

"I guess. I can hardly believe it."

Joe reached inside his book, pulled out an envelope marked "Sammy," and handed it to his great-nephew.

Sammy immediately recognized the distinctive writing on the envelope as his father's script. And without saying a word to Joe, he opened the unsealed envelope and read the letter.

Sammy,

If you're reading this letter, you have completed your agreement to run the company for a year. And while I'm certain this has not been an easy year for you, I hope and pray that the lessons learned will have been well worth it — whether or not you decide to stay. Regardless of your decision to run the company or sell it, your mother will be very well taken care of by the trust. Our attorney will continue to handle all the paperwork.

Of course, I hope that this year you learned a lot about leadership. And I'm certain if you stuck it out for a year, Uncle Joe has already given you a number of lessons about leadership. But I wanted to teach you the final lesson about leadership: **Leaders have a passion for people.**

What follows are two fundamental thoughts I have about people:

1. **Leaders value every person (employee and customer alike) as an individual.** It's not quite politically correct, but I'd even say great leaders love the people they work with. Thus, they value their relationships as the most critical aspect of their lives.

2. **Leaders try to "fit" people into the right job, not fix them.** Leaders value and respect the different strengths that everyone brings to the workplace.

And they find excellent matches in the company for all employees and the highest and best use of their strengths. By contrast, great leaders spend almost no time on trying to fix or save people.

And whether you stay with the company or leave it, what you learned this year was everything I would have wanted to teach you had I lived long enough.

I love you, son,

Dad

When Sammy finished the letter, he looked at Joe, then back at the letter. Finally he said, "Uncle Joe, I'm confused. I never questioned the first letter you showed me a year ago, but this one has, well, like I said, confused me."

Joe said nothing.

"It sounds like my father must have known that he might die unexpectedly. Is that right?"

Joe sat up and said, "Fact is that your father had a brain aneurysm."

"Did my mother know about it?"

"It's complicated."

"How so?"

Joe paused to collect his thoughts. He looked out the window for a moment and then turned toward Sammy and said, "When your father was about 55, he started to have headaches. He eventually went to the doctor after your mother and I were such nags. They found an aneurysm in his mid-brain and gave him the option of a surgery. But the location of the aneurysm was so close to other vital nerve cells that he had a 50-50 chance of becoming a vegetable. So he chose to take his chances by not having the surgery—knowing that one day, he'd just die. That might come the next day or in 20 years. Nobody, including the surgeon, was willing to bet. So your father decided not to tell your mother."

"But why? Why not? I don't understand."

"He was afraid that she'd worry herself to death. Ellen has always been a worrier."

"Yes, but not telling her. I don't understand."

"Your dad loved your mother more than anyone in the world. He thought he would protect her by not telling her. You can second-guess Sam, and I tried to convince him to tell her, but he refused and swore me to secrecy."

"What about Mom?"

"After your father's funeral and under the direction of your father's wishes, I gave your mother a letter Sam had written to her."

"And?"

"She was stunned, then angry—very angry at your father."

"I can understand that. I'm kind of angry myself right now."

"He asked your mother to wait one year to tell you himself through this letter."

"And she agreed?"

"Only after some very difficult time adjusting to this news. And believe me, she was not happy with me for holding my promise to Sam. But finally, she got through her anger, realized what Sam did was in her best interest, and agreed to wait for this letter to get in your hands."

Sammy looked up at Joe, who had a tear in his eye. Then Sammy reached over to Joe and hugged him quietly, while each cried on the other's shoulder.

Then Sammy turned to Joe and said, "I've gotta call Mom right now."

"She's at home waiting for your call."

~

Later that evening, after a tearful conversation with his mother, Sammy sat on the edge of his bed in his apartment. He read both letters that his father had written him, then neatly folded them, placed them in a plain envelope and labeled it "Dad."

Then he turned to his notebook and finished his list.

Lessons Learned

1. No one knows what they're doing until they try.

2. You get what you give. So give a little first.

3. Build trust by character, competence, caring, commitment, and consistency.

4. Change isn't easy, but if you do it right, everyone wins.

5. You have to have a vision to make it come true.

6. If you want to create a positive culture, show people by your actions what you believe in, don't just tell them.

7. Leadership is all about courage.

8. The long march begins with the first bold step.

9. Change will happen—embrace it while sticking to your core principles.

10. Leaders have a passion for people.

Epilogue

It had been a year since Sammy read his father's second letter. Uncle Joe was still doing well. Sammy visited him every weekend to read to him, tell him about how things were going at the company, talk politics, and play checkers.

Sammy and his mother, Ellen, together reconciled the issue of his father's untimely death and unexplained illness and the fact that they'd both been spared years of grief.

At the company, things had gone far better than Sammy thought they ever would. Vince got married, became a dynamic COO, and trained a new CFO. He was as content as any man alive, which Sammy loved to see. Mary decided to retire after a year of valiantly trying to absorb the culture change. Sammy had hired several new employees who had become central to his new strategic plan—based on preserving the core principles of the company while reaching out for innovations and expansion.

Based on his father's firm belief, Sammy had developed an elegantly simple corporate mission statement and had it mounted on the wall in the lobby:

Always do the right thing for the client.

He also developed a single corporate value mounted just below the mission statement:

Respect everyone **for the special gift each brings to the table.**

Lessons on Leadership

Here I would like to recount the ten leadership lessons I learned as a young Marine Corps officer during the Vietnam era. These lessons were reinforced in my careers as an FBI agent, as a faculty member and Associate Dean at the University of Virginia, and now as CEO of my own executive development company.

~

1. **No one knows what they're doing until they try.**

    At 22 years of age I flew into Vietnam, a country that I couldn't find on a map without help, hearing a language I could not speak, and fighting a war I never understood until much later in my life. Along with my duties as an artillery forward observer, I inherited a platoon of marines whose job it was to set protective fire out beyond the advancing troops, which placed me close to the enemy—a small but significant detail brushed over in basic training.

    When I stepped out of the jeep that brought me from the mortar-pocked runway in Da Nang to my first in-country assignment and walked into the hut to meet the commanding officer, I had only one thing on my mind—not to show how scared and uncertain I really was. Anything I knew came from my training at Officer Candidate School or The Basic School training at Quantico, followed by artillery training at Fort Sill, Oklahoma. Unfortunately, there is no single piece of training or manual that will prepare anyone for leadership—especially leadership in combat.

As a new leader, especially in a turbulent situation, you always look for a simple answer, a formula, or some hammer you can use to start hitting any nail as soon as your boots hit the ground. Someone—and I honestly cannot remember whether it was the captain in charge of my company in Vietnam or if it was a fellow, more senior, lieutenant—told me to "trust your instincts and do the right thing." I did that, and it worked for me. Thus, I deduced the first leadership lesson: No one knows what they're doing until they try.

As a direct corollary to this first lesson of leadership, I developed a simple mnemonic:

$$L = RT, RT, RR$$

Leaders do the Right Thing, at the Right Time, and for the Right Reason

For me, the right thing and the right time were based on my value system, my life experience, and my training. My framework for decision making revolved around our mission and the safety and well-being of the platoon. Staying true to those principles helped me every time I had a new assignment, despite how each new assignment varied from the one before it.

2. **You get what you give. So give a little first.**

If I have learned anything from my Marine Corps experience and from leading organizations over the years, it has been this: Respect others, and they will usually respect you. But, without respect, you have nothing to build a relationship on.

Because the selective service draft was in place when I joined the U.S. Marines, there was a good cross section of Americana in the military during the Vietnam War. Such variety existed even in the voluntary Marine Corps because many, like me, saw the elite Marine Corps as a better option than being drafted. In my three-year Marine Corps duty, I worked with men and women from all parts of the country. They were as varied and as different from me as any people I had ever met in college. The enlisted troops especially, who came from very different socio-economic and educational backgrounds, had good minds and hearts. As a marine leader, my job was to understand people's strengths and challenges, then be smart enough to use their strengths and shore up their challenges.

Respect is a way of accepting people as they are, not as we might want them to be. The hardest issue a leader faces is the overwhelming temptation to "fix" people and make them exactly as they—the leaders—are.

The principle of "fixing" people is fatally flawed for two reasons. First, you may not always be the best benchmark for others under your supervision, particularly in a specialized profession. And second, people don't change all that much. They come to organizations with a fully formed personality. Though you might try to modify it, you're never going to change it radically or permanently. It just doesn't work that way.

So a better approach is to work with people who come to you as they are with all of their strengths and challenges and to respect them for what they bring to the table. A simple psychological rule—the law of reciprocity—says that if you give people respect, they will want to pay you back in kind.

The research on reciprocity is clear and stark. People remember being given a gift, such as respect, kindness, and help, and they are compelled to repay at the same or at an increased level in the future. In short, you get what you give—and then some. So give a little first.

3. **Build trust by character, competence, caring, commitment, and consistency.**

    Character, strong character, has always been the fundamental requirement of the Marine Corps. I've been out of the Corps for many years now, and still, every time I either write to or speak with a marine, the term *Semper Fi* always comes up. *Semper Fi* — *Semper Fideles* (Always Faithful) is the basic character trait revered by all marines—loyal, honest, and faithful to the Corps. And in the world, this translates to being honest and loyal to the business. Indeed, *Semper Fi* is literally the slogan of the Marine Corps, the essence and foundation of character on which all other traits are based.

    Competence, or mastery of leadership skills, is essential for all marines and elegantly uncomplicated. The "keep it simple" rule always wins the day for any marine. Plain speaking and writing, clear thinking, and a mastery of all the war-fighting skills and interpersonal skills were then, and are now, the cornerstones of marine training.

    Caring about young marines is what every new officer learns to do from day one in Officer Candidate School at Quantico. Making sure every marine has the tools, the support, the peace of mind, and the team spirit he or she needs to succeed in the job is foremost in every Marine Corps officer's mind. Loyalty is not just given to a leader. It must be learned, and then earned every day.

Commitment and consistency are twin values that must be considered in tandem because one depends on the other—where you see one, you should see the other at work. First, commitment in leadership means having your head in the game—fully committing to the organization's mission, to what the organization does. In the Marine Corps, that means giving all your effort to the task at hand, without holding back. Commitment breeds loyalty and inspires commitment from those being led. People know whether or not you're in for the long haul. Once they sense your commitment, things change; relationships solidify. I think of President Harry S. Truman and the now-famous sign on his desk: "The Buck Stops Here." He led America and the world through some of its darkest hours in World War II and its aftermath, when I'm sure he could have had an easier life fishing and living in a cottage by a lake. But his personal commitment steeled the nerves of a nation perhaps not so resolute.

Consistency means remaining true to your word. In any Marine Corps leadership role, consistency is important, but in combat, it's critical for the troops to see a leader who is committed, consistent, dependable, and fair. When you're under fire, you must be able to depend on a leader who won't cut and run until the mission is completed. That doesn't mean that leaders are blinded by a single original vision and won't take in new information that might change the course of events, but it does mean they won't vacillate with every wind of doubt that blows through the battlefield.

Doing what you say you will do is not only the benchmark of good business but a fundamental benchmark of sanity itself. We consider people who bounce all over the place as "imbalanced" and unreliable. Because leaders—based on their psychological power of authority—have such an enormous effect on those being led, such leaders need to be consistent in their actions, lest they create instability in the ranks.

Good leaders bring stability and a sense of purpose to the organization. And a strong sense of commitment coupled with consistent execution produces the very ecosystem that supports and sustains the corporate organism.

4. **Change isn't easy, but if you do it right, everyone wins.**

In some ways, this lesson seems to contradict the one just before it, especially the notion of commitment and consistency. "Change is the only constant thing in life," an old professor of mine used to say. At the time I thought he was a bit of a kook, but today, many years later, I understand just how smart that professor was. In the midst of leading marines, especially in combat, leaders must be ready to adapt and change or their troops will be in constant jeopardy.

The terrain of the battlefield and of the business world are always-changing terrains. Just look at what September 11, 2001, did to the United States. In a single day, our attitude toward the threat of terrorism changed. We had to change or risk other such attacks. Politics aside, how you adapt and the speed with which you adapt become critical.

Unfortunately, change also creates growing pains. Thus, we have the inner nagging voice in all of us that wants to maintain the status quo, saying things like

Leave well enough alone.
Things are just fine.
If it isn't broke, don't fix it.

I firmly believe in studying the past as a guide to future possibilities. However, if leaders focus too much on the past, or get stuck on yesterday, they get the future they deserve—a static, polluted one.

Change must be guided by reason and leadership. Leaders set the tone for an organization, and when it comes time for change, leaders must take charge, roll up their sleeves, and dig in for the long haul. Leaders must also create an atmosphere of trust and openness among the entire team so that team members can tell the truth without recrimination, experiment without fear of failure, and know they will have the full support of their leader and the organization.

The best kind of change comes when everyone recognizes the need for it, helps set the new vision, and then works together to reach that shared vision. Great leaders are excellent at helping organizations envision a successful future. They then motivate diverse groups of people to work together for the common good of all.

The best leaders take little credit for any wins; rather, they defer such kudos to the team. As my beloved, now deceased father-in-law, Donald Sheehan, used to say, "If you don't care who gets credit, you'll be amazed at what you can get done." A brilliant leader, Don was a living example of humility. And it made everyone around him want to work on any team he led.

5. **You have to have a vision to make it come true.**

Taking objectives on the battlefield is something marines know how to do very well. In fact, most orders began with "The objective today is…." However, having the overall vision of a battle campaign is as important as knowing the near-term objectives. Leaders help organizations decide which path to follow. They contribute most by offering long-range, strategic thinking about the best markets, best products, and the best organizational structure needed for the organization to succeed.

Because such vision focuses on the future, some leaders have difficulty playing out scenarios not yet developed. In fact, picking the best future option is difficult and requires data input and analysis, thought and consideration, projection and courage. Ultimately, the CEO or unit leader must decide on the best path to take through the corporate forest. Thus, setting goals — especially large, ambitious goals — and communicating them clearly to everyone on the team leads to attaining them and succeeding. Research on goal setting bears this out. Researchers, such as Edwin Locke and his team, have concluded that 90 percent of studies involving specific, challenging goals led to higher performance than easy or no goals.

In addition to having a clear vision of the future and setting challenging and specific goals, the leader must articulate those goals to the troops. In the battlefield, because of expediency, objectives are issued orally, today even electronically via e-mail. As often as possible, a leader needs to set the new vision in writing and reinforce it with follow-up — multiple messages in multiple modes (for example, visual and audio). A clear vision, often repeated by the leader in varying modes of delivery, tends to get remembered and, more important, attained.

6. **If you want to create a positive culture, show people by your actions what you believe in, don't just tell them.**

I did not learn this lesson as concretely in basic officer training as I did from my staff sergeant—the den mother of any platoon—when I ended up in a combat unit in Vietnam. He taught me to ask first, then talk.

In combat, there's not much time to get schooled by trial and error. My sergeant, let's call him Sergeant D, took me under his wing quickly, I suspect to protect himself and the troops. He asked me a lot of questions early on, especially about how much combat experience I had. Of course, I had none, but like a good lawyer, he knew the answer to that question before he asked it. He explained that this was his "second tour in 'Nam" and that he was a career marine, not to impress me (knowing his nonchalant nature) but rather to establish quickly his bona fides and trust with me.

During my tour of duty, Sergeant D taught me, by example, to walk around and talk to the troops, get to know them, and ask them questions about their areas of expertise. However, it wasn't like we had a focus group before we executed an order. Rather, I got to understand each soldier as an individual—and each soldier's specialty, motivation, and point of view. Eventually, I got to know their strengths and challenges, when they'd had a bad day—or worse, gotten a "Dear John" (breakup) letter from someone back home. All this has helped me immensely throughout my life when the bullets began to fly—whether the bullets were "corporate shots" or real bullets.

7. **Leadership is all about courage.**

The bottom line is that leaders do the right thing at the right time for the right reason (L = RT, RT, RR). I've said this before and will repeat it again here because it's so damned important.

Under fire, marines worth their salt do the right thing at the right time and for the right reason. Combat is loaded with such examples, even when those actions involve grave personal sacrifice. Great leaders always do the right thing for the company or organization. Keeping the organization's mission foremost and personal needs secondary forces every stakeholder to have a personal stake in the common cause—creating an even better organization for tomorrow, today.

Having what I call difficult conversations with people in business takes great personal courage—to say what you, and perhaps others, think even when the circumstances are uncomfortable. I recall instances where I had to fire people—which I personally find extremely difficult because it has such a great impact on the people being fired and their families. Therefore, much thought and consideration go into such a decision, but when it's clear by everyone's account that a person may not be a good fit for the organization, it's up to the leader to tell that person the truth.

And whether it's performance appraisal time, a reprimand for a specific misdeed, or a friendly warning about inappropriate business behavior, leaders must tell the truth regardless of how difficult the conversation might feel. The payoff for such candor is almost instant relief for both parties. The conversation itself will be awkward, but the final results are far better than if the difficult conversation had been ignored. In fact, little problems that get ignored become far larger ones that eventually become potential derailers for companies and their leaders. Courage is the quickest route to comfort...even if it involves some short-term pain.

8. **The long march begins with the first bold step.**

An old Chinese philosopher, Laotzu, once said, "A journey of a thousand miles must begin with a single step." If you've ever tried to do something outside your personal comfort zone, you've felt the pressure of taking that first single step. Whether it's in our personal or professional lives, overcoming inertia — the status quo — is difficult and painful.

In the Marine Corps, tradition and steadiness are highly valued. But every commander knows that the battlefield looks a lot different than the training field and that enemies don't neatly conform to models built in training and development centers. In short, stuff happens! And leaders must be prepared for all the stuff that comes their way. So, while being rooted firmly in traditions and dependability, every marine leader is taught to adapt to the opposition. Doing anything less leads to disaster.

I think of the English fighting the colonists in the Revolutionary War. Dressed in red, easy-to-spot traditional uniforms, the English became easy targets for the insurgent, colonial revolutionaries. In Vietnam, we constantly had to adapt to the Vietcong and the North Vietnamese, or suffer grave consequences.

Here's a personal example: One day my platoon was going after the enemy on a well-trodden trail. It was an ungodly hot and humid day and we'd taken a break to rest for about 15 minutes. When I stood up, ready to take my next step, my radioman advised me to stay very still. I thought he might have spotted any one of a number of poisonous Vietnam indigenous snakes, all of which I intensely dislike.

I looked down, expecting to see a snake, and instead found my right boot under the tripwire of a homemade but highly effective and deadly booby trap, what today in Iraq is called an IED (improvised explosive device). In this case it was a grenade, the pin pulled, stuffed inside a tin can with a nearly invisible trip wire leading from it to a stake in the ground on the other side of the path. I gingerly slipped my foot out from under the tripwire. Later we blew up the grenade in place. What did I learn?

From that point on, we did not walk on such obvious paths but cut our way through the jungle, which while less popular, was ultimately far safer for everyone. Again, implementing this with the troops was difficult, but I believe in the end that it saved many lives. And I'm sure for the new guys who came to the platoon and were not there that day we found the tripwire across my foot, it was even harder to swallow this policy, despite my personal story. Nevertheless, every change is difficult, but good leaders realize that the first step is the most difficult.

9. **Change will happen—embrace it while sticking to your core principles.**

No matter what you do, change will take place—constantly. When you wake up in the morning, you're not the same person who woke up the day before. Things both large and small have changed you in often subtle but meaningful ways. Unfortunately, if you focus on this microscopic, constant change, it can lead to confusion, frustration, and inaction.

Accepting that change is constant while remembering your core values keeps you grounded enough to move forward. The three fundamental values of the Marine Corps are honor, commitment, and courage—values that marines should never abandon no matter who the enemy is. Such values are to be cherished and preserved. Similarly, the core values mentioned in this book are essentially the core values of the Corps, with some expansion: character, competence, caring, commitment, consistency—and courage.

I believe that these fundamental values provide every leader with bedrock principles of leadership that should not waver. At the same time, every marine and every leader must adapt to the changing battlefield—or the changing marketplace, respectively—which, like all of life, changes constantly.

The alternative to adaptation is extinction. Seeking new challenges and adapting to new research, techniques, and inventions become as essential as protecting bedrock values. Look at the great companies of the past 50 years—General Electric, 3M, IBM, Merck, Johnson & Johnson, and others. All have had to adapt radically to their environment, but each kept basic values that had served the company well for a number of years. Jim Collins discusses this phenomenon extensively in his books (*Good to Great* and *Built to Last*).

Simply put: All successful leadership follows a Darwinian adapt-or-die model. I'd add, however, that the fundamental values driving exceptional leaders don't change, but get applied to new situations to develop a better new world.

10. Leaders have a passion for people.

If I learned anything in the Marine Corps it was that people, not machines, made the Marine Corps work so well. All marines knew what they were expected to do. While no marine was remotely near perfect, each had real ability and talent. Some could shoot exceptionally, others could track, others could make you laugh better than Jerry Seinfeld—but everyone I've ever met in or out of the Marines has had something to teach me, whenever I was ready and willing to learn. A passion for people keeps leaders vitally interested in learning from everyone and in teaching what they know as well.

This passion for people is a central value of the Marine Corps. You'll never see it stated as such—and besides, a "passion for people" sounds a bit too new age or touchy-feely for the Marines. But I would submit that all successful marine leaders, from generals to squad leaders, have this passion, concern, and deep interest in their troops—as team members and as individuals. That concern even extends to their families and their personal interests. When you know as much as you can about marines, it's much easier for you to get them and the unit to succeed. You make fewer false starts and fewer bad decisions.

Business is no different. It's not enough to put up with people. Accept them, even embrace them on a team. I believe great leaders have to have a genuine, authentic passion for people. That comes from knowing people, what they like and dislike, their passions, ambitions, and needs; what motivates them; and where they're going. All those things make people *do* things in their lives. Those elements are collectively the soul of a person — what makes a person intrinsically who he or she is.

The great leader figures out what makes people tick and then puts them in places and jobs where they will tick the best!

Good luck and lead well.

About the Author

Dr. Steve Gladis serves as president and CEO of Steve Gladis Communications (SGC), an executive development firm focused on helping leaders achieve success. Offering executive coaching, professional development programs, and corporate consulting, SGC abides by one basic value — respect for our clients and our strategic partners. Dr. Gladis has taught hundreds of clients from a host of companies in the Northern Virginia Region, including Cox, Lockheed Martin, SAIC, Anteon, FBI, Justice, DEA, Labor, EPA, *The Washington Post*, Gannett News, and many others.

A former member of the University of Virginia's faculty, Dr. Gladis served as an Associate Dean in the School of Professional Studies and the Director of the University's Northern Virginia Center. In a previous career as an FBI special agent, he held a number of both headquarters and field-agent assignments around the country. Dr. Gladis has published numerous magazine and journal articles as well as 12 books. His next book, *The Executive Coach in the Corporate Forest,* is due to be published in the spring of 2008.

A committed civic and academic leader, Dr. Gladis serves on the Executive Board of the Fairfax County Chamber of Commerce and the Board of Directors for the Northern Virginia Community Foundation, serves on the School of Professional Studies Advisory Board at the University of Virginia, is chairman emeritus of the Board of Trustees of the Washington Math Science Technology Public Charter High School, and is a former member of the University of Virginia's Faculty Senate. He is also a former U.S. Marine Corps officer and a Vietnam veteran.